The Truth About Coffee

By Marina Kushner

Publisher's Comment: This book is not intended as a substitute for medical advice from physicians. The purpose This book has an educational purpose. It is sold with the understanding that the publisher and author shall neither be liable nor responsible for any injury caused or alleged to be caused by the information contained in this book. The reader should consult a qualified health care provider regarding his or her health. The book's contents should not be construed as medical advice. If you do not wish to be bound by the above, you may return this book to the publisher for a full refund.

Throughout this book, trademarked names are used. Rather than indicating every occurrence of a trademarked name as such, this book uses the names only in an editorial fashion and to the benefit of the trademark owner with no intention of infringement of the trademark. The author and publisher have made every effort to ensure the accuracy of the information herein. However, the information contained in this book is sold without warranty, either express or implied. Neither the authors and SCR, Inc. nor its dealers or distributors will be held liable for any damages to be caused either directly or indirectly by the instructions contained in this book or by the products described herein.

No part of this book may be reproduced or transmitted in any form or by any means, electronic or mechanical, including photocopying, recording, or by any information storage and retrieval system without written permission from the author, except for the inclusion of brief quotations in a review.

Copyright © 2014, 2009 by Marina Kushner All rights reserved
Printed in the United States of America

Library of Congress Control Number: 2008912121 Includes bibliographical references and index ISBN 978-097475825-1

Cover design by DuttonandSherman.com

ATTENTION: SCHOOLS, NON-PROFITS, AND CORPORATIONS SCR books are available at volume discounts with bulk purchases for educational, business, or sales promotional use.

For information, write to: SCR, INC 93 S. Jackson St-46673, Seattle, WA 98104

Phone: 815-642-0848 Email: scrbooks@gmail.com

TABLE OF CONTENTS

~Acknowledgments~ 1

Foreword 3

Chapter One: Kicking the Coffee Habit 5

Chapter Two: The History of Coffee 29

Chapter Three: Coffee: The Omnipresent Elixir 35

Chapter Four: The Chemistry of Coffee 39

Chapter Five: Why Women Should Avoid Coffee 49

Chapter Six: Coffee and the Central Nervous System 60

Chapter Seven: Coffee and Heart Disease 73

Chapter Eight: Do You Have the Stomach for Coffee? 81

Chapter Nine: Coffee and Cancer 87

Chapter Ten: Are You Hooked on Coffee? 101

Chapter Eleven: Breaking Free From Coffee 107

Endnotes 115

Bibliography 119

Resources 127

About The Author 129

~Acknowledgments~

First and foremost, I would like to thank my husband for his painstaking and thorough criticisms of this book. Without his support, talent, and cooperation, this book would not have been possible.

Special thanks go to my editor Patricia Ahearn, to Antoinette of Addesign-graphics.com for the superb book layout, to Joseph Sherman of DuttonandSherman.com for his excellent front cover, and to Daudesign.com for the impressive back cover.

Foreword

We currently live in a society where the coffee shop is our center for worship, and our cup of coffee has become our ultimate thirst. We fool ourselves into thinking that the only bad part of coffee is the caffeine, and we go on drinking decaf. But the evidence is striking-coffee is indeed a drug and a dangerous one.

The book you are about to read is a must for every coffee drinker and for every person who knows a coffee drinker. The facts are well laid out, and the information is presented in a very clear fashion. Coffee is dangerous and should be avoided because it causes health problems. Not only will the coffee cause havoc to your brain chemicals, but will throw your adrenal hormones into havoc.

In my organic medicine practice, I am consistently hearing patients tell me that they need their morning cup of coffee to get them going. They tell me that without their coffee, they would not be able to think clearly or have the energy to get through the day. Just like trying to get patients to stop smoking, I have to use amino acids to help my patients kick the coffee habit. But once they stop drinking their cup of java, their appetite comes back and for the first time they are able to feel energy without artificially feeling jittery.

A patient of mine recently came to see me with the complaints of migraine headaches. These headaches were becoming more and more frequent and were very disturbing for him. The first test I ran on him was a Food Sensitivity Test and that showed that his number one Food Intolerance was Coffee. He stopped drinking his one-half cup per day, and his migraines headaches disappeared.

I think we are beginning to wake up to this new reality. Just recently, Starbucks had to close several hundred stores. We have begun the search for our next magical elixir. Coffee is indeed a flavorful after dinner drink, but as the writer of this book clearly shows, comes with a cost. Coffee is notorious for making fibrocystic breast disease worse and for causing gastrointestinal upset, but coffee also is addicting and plays with our minds. We feel that we need our coffee just to open our eyes, to enjoy, while we wait for a friend to arrive, or to just pass the time we spend with ourselves. Coffee has become what cigarettes used to be—a way to pass the time.

I am confident that you will find this book a delight to read and share with others. And while there are numerous sources for you to learn about all of the different types of coffee you can drink, this is the first book of its kind to provide such a concise and comprehensive look at the truth about coffee.

After reading this book, the next time you go out to the coffee shop or grocery store or restaurant, you will begin to see coffee in a new and better light. You will no longer see coffee as just a tasty morning drink or as an after dinner delight. No, from now on, you will see coffee as the drug that it clearly is.

Craig Koniver, M.D.

Chapter One

Kicking the Coffee Habit

Millions of people are addicted to coffee, putting themselves at risk for dozens of diseases, some of which may be fatal. They need their cup of coffee just as smokers need their cigarettes. The symptoms of caffeine withdrawal can be just as painful and even longer lasting than those experienced by the most chronic alcoholics. And, just like the other junkies, dependence strips coffee addicts of their freedom. They give up their minds, bodies, and sometimes even their lives to their debilitating drug of choice: coffee.

Likewise, it could be argued that some drugs might produce more obvious diseases both mental and physical than coffee addiction does. However, coffee is the number one enemy of public's health. More people are addicted to coffee than to any other drug. No other addiction is as prevalent as coffee addiction, yet we profess to know so little about it. Lastly, there is no other addiction that has been the object of so few discussions. This spirited polemic may serve as an important one.

What Doctors Tell Us

Ask any doctor about how much coffee you can safely drink, and the answer will be, "an eight-ounce cup or two per day." Medical authorities and researchers are almost universal in their agreement that drinking any more than a couple of eight-ounce cups of coffee per day is asking for medical problems. We are talking about all kinds of coffee regardless of whether it contains caffeine or not. All kinds of coffee should be consumed in moderation. However, moderation, as we all know, means nothing when it comes to addictive beverages such as coffee. Moderation is the exception, rather than the rule, for most coffee drinkers.

According to the figures provided by the National Coffee Association of the U.S.A. Inc., the average American coffee consumer drinks 3.56 cups per day. In some sections of the country, coffee drinkers consume more than four cups per day. In other words, Americans consume, on the average, anywhere from 1.5 to 4 times more than doctors and clinicians say is safe. And remember, that is the average. Millions of Americans drink a great deal more than the average.

Researchers often find that coffee consumers drink from 10 to 20 cups of coffee per day. Many professional researchers confirm what informal surveys often reveal: millions of people are addicted to coffee. A government study shows that at least 68,240,000 Americans drink 3 cups of coffee or more every day. At least 30 million drink 5 or more cups per day. Some 21 million drink 6 or more cups of coffee per day.

Thus, the gravity of the problem is as enormous as it is shocking. Millions of people drink coffee in amounts that greatly exceed doctor-recommended levels. Millions of people drink coffee excessively and addictively, thereby doubling, tripling, or even quadrupling their exposure to illness and disease. The mental and physical wounds caused by coffee addiction are staggering, but as often happens, we learn too little, too late to prevent harm.

Innocent Beginnings

Coffee drinkers begin their precipitous descent from novices to addicts innocently enough. For most people, starting the day with a morning eye-opener of hardy black coffee is routine. This so-called ritual may be repeated once or, perhaps, twice during the day.

For hundreds of years, we have praised coffee's ability to promote rapid and clear thinking, to improve intellectual efforts, and enhance mental acuity – all valued attributes in a society that worships success and achievement. How can something that seems so right be so wrong?

Coffee is an addictive substance that is toxic in large doses. We develop a tolerance to coffee, as to any other addictive substance, and increase our dosages because lower amounts no longer work as well. However, excessive coffee consumption causes damage to our health.

The typical coffee consumer drinks a couple of cups each day without an incident. This habit usually begins in response to social or peer group pressure or as part of family socialization. The vast majority of coffee consumers who remain at low levels of a cup or two each day have only occasional complaints: a sleepless night here and there, an upset stomach once in a while, or a headache.

Most doctors would agree that coffee consumption at levels of one or two cups a day poses no significant health hazard. However, millions of coffee drinkers, like millions of tobacco smokers and alcohol consumers, do not stop at just one or two. They go on and on, often with devastating results.

Who knows the reason why? Who knows why some people can experiment with drugs and leave them behind while others continue to make them a major and debilitating part of their lives?

The answer may lie in the biochemistry of an individual. People with low serotonin levels have poor self-control and compulsive behaviors, which result in addictions, such as overeating, chain smoking, excessive coffee consumption, and drugs. Coffee, due to its addictive nature, makes them even more compulsive; they just do not stop drinking cup after cup. The biochemical imbalance that causes poor self-control and compulsive behaviors may happen if the serotonin neurotransmitter system lacks a sufficient amount of tryptophan, an essential amino acid.

Coffee: A Mild Legal Drug

People say that they enjoy the taste of coffee, and the agreeable taste keeps them coming back for more. Other coffee consumers talk about the great "pick-me-up" that coffee gives them, how it arouses their sleepy brains and spurs them into action in the morning. During the day, their mental acuity and alertness is heightened with more coffee. It is part of the coffee break ritual, the great social lubricant of any work-place. So why does one decide to quit? Obviously the disadvantages of coffee drinking begin to outweigh the advantages.

Thus, people begin drinking coffee because they enjoy its effects, but then they quit because they become fed up with coffee's harmful effects. But we also have a scientific puzzle: why do coffee drinkers escalate from the lower, enjoyable levels of coffee consumption to the higher, unenjoyable levels? What causes them to slide into addiction?

Coffee and Your Brain

Dr. Karlis Ullis, an author of the book *Age Right,* explains that there are three main neurotransmitters in the brain: acetylcholine, which is responsible for our memory, language, speech, and thoughts; serotonin, which is responsible for our emotional state, sleep, appetite, cravings, and obsessive-compulsive behaviors, such as overeating and abusing different kinds of drugs; and dopamine, which is responsible for energy level, vigilance, alertness, reaction time, emotional highs, spontaneity, as well as our addiction to stimulants.[1] Stimulation of the dopamine system also increases heartbeat, rate of breathing, and involuntary movements, such as blinking. The latter may explain why some coffee addicts suffer from eyelid twitching.

The majority of people prefer coffee as their stimulant of choice because it provides a quick release of dopamine, which increases their energy levels and emotional highs. They feel fixed due to enhanced dopamine levels. Without their drug, coffee consumers feel mentally and physically drained.

The drawback of using coffee as a stimulant is that it is an addictive stimulant, and therefore, you may consume too much. It often feels like you cannot get enough of it. However, excessive coffee consumption has negative effects on dopamine-producing brain cells. It over stimulates, depletes, and leads to the degeneration of the dopamine neurons.

The number of dopamine-producing cells we have declines with age, regardless of whether we use heavy drugs and stimulants. There are other factors that may cause the destruction of these vulnerable neurons, among which are exposure to heavy metals, noxious fumes, and lack of sleep. However, cocaine, speed, ephedrine, coffee, and other drugs and stimulants accelerate dopamine depletion. Severe depletion of dopamine neurons is known as Parkinson's disease.

Coffee drinkers tend to defend their lifestyle choice. Thus, they report that there are some studies indicating that coffee is beneficial. Asthmatics convince you that coffee helps them with breathing; others say it is beneficial for those who suffer from Parkinson's disease. They are right because coffee stimulates dopamine release; however, excessive coffee consumption depletes the system.

In the case of Parkinson's, coffee is not significantly helpful because approximately 70 to 80 percent of dopamine neurons are irreversibly lost before the symptoms of the disease, such as slow movements and reaction time, overly stiff posture, shuffling, and lack of facial expression, become noticeable. However Parkinson's is not the only disease we need to worry about. Not everyone develops this condition regardless of declining levels of dopamine.

With age, the body releases less of not just dopamine, but also, acetylcholine and norepinephrine, too, as well as certain hormones, such as sex, growth, thyroid, and melatonin, leading to an imbalance within the entire system. If we have not yet lost all of our acetylcholine neurons (complete depletion of which is characterized by Alzheimer's disease) and the capacity to make reasoned decisions, why would we willingly and voluntarily choose to speed up our own aging process by using narcotics and stimulants.

The Quiet Storm

Regardless of the reasons why, as coffee intake begins to climb, so does the pain, the suffering, the illness, and the disease. Unfortunately, the buildup is so gradual that the causal relationship between coffee consumption and illness is often difficult to define or is undetectable. The coffee addict cannot determine the link.

Coffee's toxic effect on the body is extremely varied from person to person. Some people are very susceptible to its adverse effects, whereas others are only slightly affected. The factors of this wide-ranging variance include age, weight, metabolism, gender, and a level of tolerance to coffee.

Drug Tolerance

Tolerance is an adaptation to a drug that is taken regularly. Tolerance is inherent in most drug use, whereby the pharmacological effect of the drug becomes less significant over time. This is the reason why increasingly larger doses are needed to obtain the same effect. This is the reason why heroin users build up $1,000-a-week habits, smokers light up a couple of packs of cigarettes a day, and coffee addicts drink five or more cups per day.

Tolerance develops when a drug is taken regularly, which attenuates its effect and leads to a gradual increase in dosage. Coffee drinkers often develop tolerance and need to increase their doses of caffeine, either through an increased number of cups per day or by preparing a stronger brew.

Caffeine is a psychoactive drug that can lead to chronic tolerance. Studies show that tolerance can develop to some but not necessarily all of the effects of a substance. Thus, tolerance can develop to some but not all of the effects of caffeine: daily consumption of a cup of coffee eventually will not produce the same stimulation or locomotor effects as it did initially.

Gradually developing tolerance to the habitual daily amount of coffee leads to caffeine abuse and dependence because larger doses are needed to achieve the desired effect. One or two cups do not satisfy as before, because they do not produce the same effect. This leads to an increase in strength, number, and size of cups of coffee consumed by the addict.

Chronic coffee consumers who have built up a considerable tolerance to this drug find it extremely difficult to satisfy their cravings with smaller doses. Heavy coffee consumers have built up such a tremendous level of tolerance that they cannot realize that they are in trouble.

For coffee consumers with a low tolerance, drinking the same amount of coffee as those who are seriously addicted to it do would undoubtedly cause tremors and jitters or even delirium and hallucinations.

The opportunities for coffee abuse are everywhere, occurring every day with regularity as predictable as sunrises and coffee breaks. The price we pay for our addiction is all the more staggering because we, addicts, are often unwitting victims.

Coffee Affects the Brain

Coffee is a substance that produces changes in the brain, causing tolerance, dependence, and addiction.

Just as with illegal stimulants, excessive coffee consumption leads to brain condition that is characterized by physical, mental, and emotional dependence, in this case on caffeine.

Daily stimulation affects the process of neurotransmission (the way neurons communicate with each other). Excessive caffeine consumption forces the neurotransmitters to work beyond their norms. It is destructive to the brain and leads to alterations in cellular structure, possibly causing behavioral abnormalities and serious psychological changes.

Coffee is a mild narcotic because it contains caffeine, a psychotropic substance that is toxic in large doses. Habitual use of psychoactive substances causes changes on the cellular level, which affect normal brain function and, therefore, emotional state and behavior.

Coffee is a stimulant that enhances dopamine activity. It changes the way we feel, think, and behave because it affects dopamine neurons. While coffee initially increases dopamine activity, the constant stimulation eventually leads to dopamine depletion or loss of responsiveness to dopamine.

Stimulants that enhance dopamine activity (caffeine is one of them) temporarily elevate mood, cause excitement, or even induce a state of euphoria. When the effect of caffeine wears off, however, there is usually a "crash."

The long-term effect of the constant stimulation is detrimental to the brain and body and can lead to numerous mental and physical disorders. The long-term use of stimulants and constantly heightened dopamine activity can cause anxiety, panic attacks, and hyperactivity. Coffee addicts may have poor memory and reduced cognitive ability. Coffee and other stimulants disrupt sleep cycles, which also can affect memory. The brain ages faster.

Addiction and Withdrawal

Addiction is a chronic psychic disorder, which is characterized by the daily need to take a drug and physical and mental disturbances that are caused by the drug itself. Although genetic predisposition accounts for 50 percent of addiction, the daily use of psychoactive drugs has the potential to lead to dependence in anyone. Thus, everyday coffee drinking will inevitably cause caffeine addiction in most people, due to its physically addictive effects as well as the factors causing psychological dependence.

Coffee will become a daily necessity for most consumers because their brain will inevitably demand caffeine, but the level of addiction may depend on genetic, environmental, and psychological characteristics. The earlier in life a person begins drinking coffee, the higher his chances of becoming seriously addicted to caffeine and the more severe the symptoms of caffeine withdrawal can manifest.

Coffee addicts typically depend on their drug of choice not only physically but also psychologically. Even the thought of a cup of coffee can cause an emotional lift. Anticipation of the morning coffee ritual induces pleasure and becomes the moving force that pushes the coffee addict out of the bed.

Drinking coffee is the most popular method to deliver caffeine into the body. Caffeine is a mild drug in comparison with illegal psychoactive substances. However, just as with other psychoactive substances, caffeine causes withdrawal symptoms.

Withdrawal is a sign and result of physical dependence. Although caffeine is considered mildly addictive, and most coffee addicts recover after three or four days, some go through severe withdrawal for weeks and even months. The biochemical changes in the central and autonomic nervous systems induced by coffee addiction can cause negative emotions, fatigue, cravings, headaches, sleep disorders, problems with concentration, short-term memory issues, and difficulty making decisions, even after the actual caffeine withdrawal is over. Thus, for some coffee addicts it can be long and painful process of recovery, during which they can relapse.

Coffee is a legal stimulant, and therefore, recovering addicts encounter temptations practically everywhere. This makes it difficult to quit. Since coffee is readily available and almost everyone is drinking it (many seemingly without problems), the addict may not withstand temptations and justify his relapse.

Withdrawal symptoms can be weak or severe, depending on the amount of coffee the addict consumes. However, nearly all addicts experience cravings for a cup in the morning because the level of caffeine in the blood drops during the night. The morning discomfort, dizziness, drowsiness, sluggishness, headaches, irritability, and shakes are signs of physical dependence and caffeine withdrawal. The symptoms of caffeine withdrawal cause cravings and distress, and therefore, coffee drinkers cannot start their day without a cup.

Coffee and Allergy

Excessive caffeine consumption can have deleterious effects on everyone, but these effects may vary.

Some people are extremely sensitive to caffeine. Others do not experience any side effects, but may develop mental and physical disorders later in life. Still others are actually allergic to caffeine, although they may not be aware of it.

The allergic reaction, known as anaphylaxis, can have mild or severe mental and physical manifestations, which can progress over the years. Depending on the amount of caffeine consumed daily, the symptoms can range from skin rash, eczema, agitation, palpitations, chest pain, nervousness, forgetfulness, muscle tension, and blurred vision to cognitive and mental manifestations, such as unreasonable and strange behavior, confusion, irritability, mood swings, difficulty concentrating or making decisions, paranoia, hallucinations, anxiety attacks, and dementia.

Coffee and Mental Illness

Sometimes symptoms of caffeine allergy can be diagnosed as psychosis, bipolar disorder, depression, attention deficit disorder, or schizophrenia. There are psychiatrists who agree that some patients who suffer from mental disorders might not need any other treatment besides discontinuation of caffeine consumption. There are many cases of remission.

Caffeinism is not frequently diagnosed, however, it might afflict millions of people. In extreme cases, excessive caffeine consumption can lead to paranoid delusion. Some patients in mental wards might not be there if they were not addicted to caffeine.

A study conducted in 60 hospitals found that approximately 40 percent of patients consumed excessively large doses of caffeine.[2] The researchers concluded that excessive caffeine consumption must be taken into consideration during the diagnosis of mental disorders.

Excessive coffee consumption may also cause psychological disorders by depleting the body of vitamin B-6, which is essential for the production of serotonin. Low levels of serotonin are found in people who suffer from depression and anxiety. Since caffeine suppresses appetite, coffee drinkers may have poor nutrition, which only exacerbates the problem.

In 1994, caffeine was included in the Diagnostic and Statistical Manual of Mental Disorders (DSMM). Caffeine is also included in the International Statistical Classification of Diseases and Related Health Problems.

Are You in Trouble?

Coffee addiction is not a matter of how much you drink, but rather, the effect it has on your mind and body. You can drink just one cup a day, and you may experience withdrawal symptoms as soon as you open your eyes the next morning, such as headaches, sluggishness, irritability, and a burning desire for a hot cup of coffee, which compels you to get up. And therein lies the problem: you, as most coffee addicts, do not know that you are an addict.

The biggest delusion and justification among coffee drinkers is that coffee helps them to wake up in the morning. In reality, no one needs coffee to wake up. Those who do not consume coffee wake up fresh, alert, and energetic without it. Coffee drinkers, however, need their morning doses because their blood levels of caffeine drop during the night and they begin to experience its withdrawal symptoms. They need their drug and do not realize that this seemingly unbreakable dependence can be eliminated in approximately two or three weeks, which is the average amount of time that is needed to change practically any habit.

Excuse me for touching on such a delicate theme, but another popular reason for using coffee in the morning is that it is an excellent diuretic. However, with every cup of coffee the body loses two to three cups of water and excretes certain vitamins and minerals, such as B12, C, calcium, magnesium, iron, and potassium. From the medical position, to be dependent on stimulants is detrimental to one's health. The large intestine can and should work on its own. Instead of relying on caffeine, it is better to consume high-fiber foods – bran, whole grains, kiwi, figs, prunes, beets are excellent sources – and drink plenty of water. Three or four cups of celery juice also cleanse the intestinal tract just as effectively as caffeine does. For the intestinal stimulation in the morning, coffee can also be replaced with a couple of cups of hot water (with lemon juice or without). If your diet is rich in fiber, you will be satisfied with the results.

The drawback of using coffee as a diuretic is that sooner or later you will increase your dose. You may still drink the same amount of coffee, but you will prepare a progressively stronger brew in order to feel satisfied. Thus, by increasing your coffee intake, you increase your health risk.

Excessive coffee consumption also dehydrates the body. With every cup of coffee the body loses water, dehydrating the cells, especially the digestive juices, bile, and blood. Dehydration is also one of the reasons why heavy coffee drinkers suffer from headaches.

Some addicts cannot recognize the pathological disturbances caused by coffee. Irritability and mood swings, for example, are often symptoms of addiction. The addict himself may not recognize these symptoms as symptoms of caffeine addiction because he believes that these behaviors are merely facets of his personality. Family and friends may also not realize that coffee is a mood-altering substance.

A woman may not relate a condition of which she is aware to her coffee intake, whether excessive or not. For example, she may realize that she has lumps in her breasts but is unaware that they may be a result of her coffee intake.

Many coffee drinkers report that they suffer from severe stomach pains and believe that the discomfort is caused by their coffee consumption. However, because they also enjoy drinking coffee, they refuse to quit.

The situations above are not unlike those of other substance abusers, particularly alcoholics. Many alcoholics are unaware that they have a drinking problem and are equally unaware of the alcohol's effect on their minds and bodies. However, many alcoholics are aware of their addiction but will not, or cannot, do anything about it. They are completely dependent.

Worse yet, both coffee drinkers and alcoholics share the need for self-protective armor. They tend to minimize and underestimate both their intake and its effect on their minds and bodies, a rationalization that helps perpetuate their dependence.

What to Expect

Coffee has negative effects on the mind and body, both short and long term. We can see how this beverage disrupts the central nervous system (CNS) every day. Coffee is such a powerful stimulant that the entire body is virtually under its control. Depending on the amount consumed, coffee drinkers experience nervousness, headaches, tremors, visual flashes, hyperesthesia, insomnia, impaired concentration, increased agitation, irritability, and mood swings. These symptoms of central nervous system disturbance are so prevalent in our society that they became known as "coffee nerves."

It would be disturbing enough if coffee nerves were all we had to cope with as a result of our addiction. However, there are several more—some of which are fatal—pathologies.

Coffee can create such a strain on the heart that it should be no surprise that heart disease has been linked to coffee consumption. Coffee's effect on the cardiovascular system can be recorded in the systemic, coronary, and cerebral circulation patterns. Following coffee ingestion, the coronary arteries, the pulmonary and the general systemic vessels become dilated, which results in an increased flow of the blood to the heart muscle and a decreased flow to the brain by constricting the cerebral blood vessels. Thus, any abnormalities can strike the heart.

Research has shown that an abnormally fast heartbeat (tachycardia) occurs, as well as a slower than normal heartbeat (bradycardia), extra contractions between heartbeats (extrasystole), an irregular heart beat (arrhythmia), abnormally low blood pressure (hypotension), and abnormally high blood pressure (hypertension).

Excessive coffee consumption can lead to chronic CNS disturbances, palpitations, headaches, skin problems, and sleep disorders. These are just a few of the short-term effects of coffee addiction. The prognosis for the long term may be the matter of life and death. Coffee addiction can lead to stomach ulcers, kidney stones, birth defects, and other pathologies.

Excessive coffee consumption has been linked to heart disease and certain forms of cancer, such as pancreas, bladder, liver, and lungs. Women may experience breast cancer, fibrocystic disease, miscarriages, stillbirths, and other problems. Since caffeine affects hormonal processes in the body, it can potentially hinder breast development in young women. Children, because they weigh less than adults, are especially sensitive to the effects of coffee. The elderly, more keenly aware of mental and physical disturbances, are often the victims of sleepless nights and jittery days because of a coffee overdose.

Coffee often interferes with prescribed drugs. Thus, caffeine may cancel the pharmacological effect of another drug. This problem has been reported in hospitals, clinics, and mental wards.

Some medications can have serious toxic effects on the liver, especially when taken with alcohol or caffeine. According to researchers at the University of Washington, who published a study on Chemical Research in *Toxicology* in October 2007, the pain reliever acetaminophen, which contains caffeine, can be highly toxic to the liver.

More abnormalities are evident in the gastrointestinal system. Coffee consumption can cause nausea, vomiting, diarrhea, epigastric pain, peptic ulcers, and diuresis. These ailments are prevalent regardless of whether the coffee you drink is regular or decaffeinated.

Some of the digestive and gastrointestinal problems associated with regular coffee consumption do not disappear when one switches to decaf. Decaffeinated coffee can induce heartburn and acid reflux. Researchers have also found that decaffeinated coffee prevents the body from absorbing certain minerals, such as iron, calcium, and magnesium.

Coffee has been found to have a definite impact on the gallbladder. Either regular or decaffeinated coffee induces contractions of the gallbladder that may cause pain to those who suffer from gallstone disease.

In all likelihood, as a coffee drinker, you are probably already too familiar with some of these annoying and painful conditions from your own experience. You have had that drugged up hyper feeling. You have probably had sleepless nights, headaches, nausea, and stomach pains. Perhaps you have even had stomach ulcers, rosacia, palpitations, or breast tumors. Well, if you continue drinking coffee, it is quite possible that the distressing symptoms you now have will intensify. With increased coffee intake, you may develop dangerous diseases. Such is the prognosis for consumers of this hazardous, addictive stimulant.

Coffee and the Gallbladder

The gallbladder, which is located under the liver, stores bile that is produced by the liver for digesting fat. Bile is released through the bile duct to the small intestine when needed. When gallstones block the bile flow, this process is painful.

Gallstone disease is common among women, older people, and those who are overweight. Surgical removal of the gallbladder is a common procedure for people prone to frequent gallstone attacks.

However, studies show that in some cases people experience pain even after the gallbladder has been removed. This has led researchers to conclude that gallstone attacks might be reactions to certain foods, such as eggs, meat and dairy products, citrus fruits, and caffeine-containing beverages. Thus, those who have gallbladder or liver problems should limit or avoid coffee, as well as white sugar and flour products, fried foods, and even chocolate.

Coffee Affects the Skin

Our health disorders reflect on the face. Those who consume too much coffee often have unhealthy-looking skin, because caffeine can have a significant impact on the skin. Caffeine dehydrates the body, decreasing the skin moisture. It is also stimulates the sweat glands, which can produce too much oil and clog the pores.

Caffeine stimulates the adrenal glands and leads to overproduction of stress hormones, which are toxic in excess and have a significant effect on the endocrine system. Coffee also contains other toxic chemicals that affect the body. Overproduction of stress hormones leads to hormonal imbalance and illnesses of the endocrine and nervous systems.

The hormonal imbalance caused by emotional stress, excessive coffee consumption, or other stimulants leads to a decline in production of DHEA, melatonin, and other hormones. Thus, there is a connection between premature aging and excessive coffee consumption. Drinking too much coffee can speed up the aging process. Uneven skin tone, redness, acne, itchiness, excessive oiliness or dryness can also be a result of hormonal imbalance caused by drinking too much coffee.

Coffee and Seborrheic Dermatitis

Seborrheic dermatitis is characterized by the constant formation of dry skin scales. The cause of seborrheic dermatitis is unknown; however, research shows that excessive coffee consumption is one of the factors that can lead to this type of eczema, which affects the sebaceous glands. High levels of caffeine over stimulate and create imbalance in the body that can cause sebaceous glands to uncontrollably discharge excessive amounts of oil. This is most noticeable on the face, though the scalp, neck, chest, and back can be affected because the sebaceous glands are also active in these areas. Research literature notes a number of instances in which skin lesions appear and disappear in response to coffee consumption.

A 55-year-old man from North Dakota told researchers that he drank coffee because "it was something to do with my hands," but he quit because of a lesion on his face that simply never healed. The lesion appeared as a scaly patch next to his nose and under his eye. The doctor diagnosed the ailment as seborrhea, an excess discharge from the sebaceous glands.

The man drank about five cups of coffee daily for some forty years before he quit. "I had a lesion on my face, and I experimented with dropping various things from my diet. When I quit drinking coffee, the lesion went away. It was gone just like that. I'm definite on that. It was caused by my coffee drinking, and the scales disappeared so dramatically when I quit," he said.

Another respondent in the same survey, a woman of 22, reported an identical experience. She had been drinking about two to three cups of coffee a day for about five years before she became concerned about cancer. She had no other reason to quit, but when she did, she was amazed that a skin lesion around her nose miraculously disappeared. She had suffered from the scaly facial blemish for years, but since she quit, it has never reappeared.

Powdery or greasy scales on the face cause great distress to millions of coffee drinkers. If only they knew how easily they could treat themselves.

Coffee Overdose

There has never been a reported case of fatality from drinking too much coffee. However, the BBC news reported a case of a teenage girl who was hospitalized after she began to experience palpitations, difficulty in breathing, and fever after she drank seven double espressos.[3]

According to the Starbucks' website, a single one-ounce espresso contains 75 mg of caffeine. This means that the girl had consumed 1,050 mg of caffeine, but since espresso is a highly concentrated beverage, she had consumed only 14 ounces of coffee, slightly more than a 12-ounce can. If she had consumed more, she could possibly have died of a heart attack due to a caffeine overdose. Thus, we cannot completely dismiss the possibility of fatality. There is also one well-known incident: a French writer Honore de Balzac died from a coffee overdose, although besides drinking coffee, he used to chew whole coffee beans, which probably was the cause of his death. One coffee bean contains 20 mg of caffeine therefore a lethal overdose is quite possible.

However, cases of coffee overdoses are not common for several reasons. First, chewing coffee beans is not a common habit. Second, coffee is quickly metabolized and excreted, and therefore, it is almost impossible to reach a lethal dose by drinking coffee. Third, drinking so much coffee is likely to cause extreme vomiting, reducing its amount in the body.

However, this does not mean that people cannot actually die from a coffee overdose. Coffee overdoses are uncommon only because the cardiac tolerance to caffeine is greater when it delivered through beverage consumption than it would be via pills or intravenously and also because no one drinks so much coffee to reach a lethal dose, which is approximately 70 eight-ounce cups of regular or 40 of gourmet style coffee, although it may be much less for women and children because its effect depends on body weight.

However, drinking even several cups of coffee daily can cause damage to the brain and body, which can progress over the years and lead to serious and possibly fatal diseases.

Coffee and Adrenal Fatigue

Coffee increases stress hormone production, which depletes the adrenal glands. Just one cup of coffee is enough to trigger the brain (pituitary glands) to send a message to the adrenal glands to release the stress hormones – adrenaline, noradrenaline, and cortisol – to the bloodstream.

Stress hormones release results in a feeling of a sudden blood rush, which we usually experience in a stressful or dangerous situation. The jolt we get from coffee is actually a stress hormone rush. Coffee is a strong stimulant and an irritant that triggers the body's defense response by releasing the stress hormones. However, eventually, this defense mechanism weakens.

Those who consume too much coffee practically run on adrenaline. The energy that comes after a cup of coffee is in large part the release of stress hormones and stored blood glucose, accompanied by the potentially dangerous increase in blood pressure. Excessive production of stress hormones can have a detrimental effect on the mind and body.

The constant artificial adrenaline pumping through the use of coffee exhausts the glands to the point that they do not secrete enough hormones. Looking to experience the former adrenaline jolt, a coffee addict begins to increase his intake, placing more pressure on the glands, which cannot cope with the addict's demands. This cycle cannot continue without consequences.

Sooner or later, coffee addicts develop adrenal depletion. Everyday overproduction of stress hormones, which are toxic in excess, eventually changes the blood composition, which, in turn, negatively affects the proper function of the immune, endocrine, and nervous systems, which can lead to chronic fatigue, increased blood sugar and insulin levels, weight gain, increased blood pressure, irritability, anxiety, depression, insomnia, frequent viral outbreaks, ulcers, thinning of the skin, bone loss, thyroid problems, and other disturbing signs of health deterioration.

Coffee and the Liver

Excessive coffee consumption leads to overstimulation and exhaustion not only of the adrenal glands but also the pancreas and the liver. The exhausted liver cannot detoxify the blood properly and therefore the unfiltered overload of toxins circulates throughout the body, poisoning tissues and leading to various diseases.

When the liver does not work properly, impurities may also exit through the skin, which is itself a detoxifying organ. Skin issues may be the sign of a sluggish, congested liver – the result of drinking too much coffee, as well as of using other drugs and stimulants.

Dark spots on the skin, high cholesterol, gallbladder disease, constipation, irritable bowels, and even premature gray hair (a problem of mineral absorption) are also indicators that the liver is not working well.

Coffee and Kidney Stones

There are four types of kidney stones. The most commonly occurring type involves calcium buildup, which forms the stones. The second type of stones forms from magnesium and ammonia, the latter is a by-product of protein utilization. Uric acid stones, the third type, form as a result of acid accumulation, usually in people who consume meat or other acid-forming foods in large amounts. The fourth type is cystine stones. These stones are rare and mostly hereditary form.

Excessive consumption of coffee may play a significant role in the formation of calcium stones, the most common type of kidney stones. A study conducted at Washington State University, Spokane, showed that caffeine significantly increases calcium levels in the urine.[4]

Two groups of participants (one comprised of subjects predisposed to stone formations, the other not predisposed) consumed nothing but caffeine and water; the level of calcium in their urine was measured two hours before and after caffeine intake. The test also showed significantly increased levels of magnesium, sodium, and citrate in both groups of participants.

The study concluded that excessive accumulation of calcium and sodium in the urine increases the risk of stone formation. Other researchers theorize that caffeine is not the main cause but a major contributor to stone formation. Excessive consumption of caffeine not only increases calcium in the urine but also leads to dehydration, another significant factor in stone formation.

Coffee and the Eyes

Excessive coffee consumption not only increases blood pressure, both systolic and diastolic, but also intraocular – that is, eye pressure. Can it be dangerous? Yes, it can.

Increased intraocular pressure constricts the optic nerve and restricts blood flow, which brings oxygen and nutrients to the eye, gradually damaging nerve cells that are necessary for vision. Eye pressure can cause permanent damage to the optic nerve. Increased eye pressure raises the risk for developing glaucoma. Untreated glaucoma can lead to blindness.

At the University of Benin in Nigeria, a study was conducted to ascertain the effects of coffee on the eyes.[5] The study involved two groups of volunteers. One group of healthy participants, ages 20 to 27, drank regular coffee; the other group drank decaffeinated. The researchers periodically measured intraocular pressure in both groups of participants.

The study found that regular coffee increases intraocular pressure, which was elevated for several minutes after consumption of coffee, although the amount of time differed among the participants of the group. It also demonstrated an increase in blood pressure, both systolic and diastolic, in the group of the participants who consumed regular coffee. The group that consumed decaffeinated coffee did not show pressure elevation – neither blood nor intraocular.

Coffee and Your pH Balance

Coffee, whether regular or decaffeinated, can harmfully affect the body's acid-alkaline balance (pH). In general, some foods produce acid metabolic reaction in the body; the others create alkaline reaction. Thus, all meats, eggs, dairy, and flour products, as well as alcoholic and coffee beverages, produce an acid reaction in the body, whereas fruits, vegetables, some nuts, and most seeds are alkaline-forming foods.

Your dietary preferences play an important role in the proper safe-guarding of your pH balance and therefore your health. Overconsumption of acid-producing foods and beverages raises the level of acidity in the body. If not enough alkali is obtained through the diet to neutralize the acid, the body is forced to use its own mineral reserves from the bones, teeth, and other tissues, and as a result, weaken their structure.

The body eliminates the excess of metabolic acids through the kidneys, lungs, and skin, but its eliminating capacity has certain limits per day. If too much acid-forming foods are consumed daily, the body fails to neutralize acids properly. Thus, we develop acidosis, a condition that is characterized by excessive accumulation of acids in the body.

Chronic acid overload can gradually and imperceptibly bring you to an early grave. Health deterioration begins on the cellular level with the following disorders of all tissues, organs, and systems in the body, which starts in the most vulnerable places, weaken from birth or by an illness. The body, including the brain, cannot function properly in the high-acid state. Only bacteria, fungi, and viruses proliferate and thrive in the acid bodily environment.

An acid overload impairs the body's ability to produce energy, both mental and physical. Lack of energy grows in direct proportion with the acid overload, eventually leading to chronic fatigue. The more acids you accumulate, the less energy you have. The less energy you have, the more coffee you consume. The more coffee you consume, the more acid you produce, and therefore, the less energy you have. This merry-go-round never stops.

However, we can unquestionably increase our energy levels, avoid various health problems, and prevent life-threatening diseases if we include more alkalizing foods in our diets and reduce consumption of acid-forming foods and beverages. Thus, we can maintain the body's normal acid-alkaline balance.

Coffee Carries a Risk of Stroke

Some heavy coffee drinkers are unaware that they live on the edge of a constant risk of stroke. About three to six percent of people in the U.S. at any given time have a brain aneurysm – an abnormal bulge in the wall of an artery. This condition does not cause any symptoms until it begins to progress, to leak blood or to rupture. Most people are undiagnosed and have no idea they are living with this risk.

If brain aneurysm is not corrected by surgery or treatment, it can grow and weaken the arterial wall, which can burst under high blood pressure and cause bleeding in the brain that leads to stroke. In the U.S., this happens approximately 25,000 to 30,000 times each year, with 40 percent of these incidents ending in death.

Aneurysm rupture can be triggered by simple ordinary day-to-day activities such as exercise, sex, blowing the nose, defecation with strain, use of illegal drugs, and consumption of alcoholic and caffeine-containing beverages. It also can be triggered by anger, shock, and major emotional stress.

The primary common risk factor behind these varied causes of aneurysm rupture is a temporary increase in blood pressure. Research shows that drinking coffee represents the highest risk of all the activities listed, since its high level of caffeine causes an increase in blood pressure.

The triggering stroke factors in people with brain aneurysm were determined by researchers from the University Medical Center in Utrecht, Netherlands, who studied the cases of 250 aneurysm rupture survivors.[6] The study concluded that a temporary increase in blood pressure could cause brain aneurysm rupture, which results in severe headache, stiff neck, nausea, vomiting, loss of consciousness, and stroke. Thus, drinking coffee, especially in large amounts, increases the risk of stroke in people with brain aneurysm.

How Can This Be?

It has been many years since the U.S. Surgeon General issued his famous report linking smoking to cancer, heart disease, and a wide variety of pathological phenomena. In 1964, there were approximately 53 million in the United States who smoked. Since then, more than 50 million Americans have stopped smoking, but because of population increases, more than 54 million people still smoke.

Thousands of studies have implicated smoking in higher death rates, and yet millions still smoke. How can this be? They either do not believe or do not care that they will be stricken with any one of a half-dozen forms of cancer, several types of heart disease and stroke, emphysema, or a plethora of other ailments, just from smoking cigarettes. They simply do not believe or they rationalize.

The Unbelievers

This really should not surprise us. Many people can carry their doubts regarding pathological cause and effect to its ultimate and deadly conclusion. They have to test for themselves whether the predictions are true or false, and more importantly, they must determine if it will hold true for them.

It has been proven beyond a shadow of a doubt that smoking dramatically shortens people's lifespan through cancer, heart disease, emphysema, and a number of other ailments. And still, millions refuse to believe, even when confronted face-to-face with overwhelming evidence.

At the University of Minnesota, hundreds of men and women participated in a voluntary research project that sought to determine whether high-risk heart attack patients would, or even could, mend their lifestyles and lower their at-risk status.

All of the participants smoked cigarettes, were overweight, and had high cholesterol levels. All were prime candidates for heart attacks.

Their sessions consisted of weekly meetings, dietary and weight reduction counseling, smoking cessation programs, and other informational seminars.

Most participants who took the program to heart had improved their health by changing their lifestyles. Those who did not, died.

The Grim Prognosis

As researchers turn their clinical gaze to coffee with keener, more knowledgeable eyes, more pathologies, some of them fatal, are likely to be inextricably linked to its consumption. The scenario will undoubtedly blaze the same trail as smoking did, which was first associated with, and then proven to be, a major contributing factor to cancer and heart disease. However, as we can see, knowledge does not stop everyone.

As with millions of smokers, coffee addicts are still undecided on a course of action. Some believe that coffee is absolutely safe, and they will continue to swill cup after cup, day after day. However, a growing number of coffee consumers are giving it up entirely. They are far ahead of researchers, medical authorities, and the government. They have realized through self-diagnosis and subsequent self-prescription that coffee consumption is dangerous to their health. They are not health nuts. They are just people who have recognized that this seemingly innocuous beverage is harmful to their minds and bodies. You will realize this as well.

Chapter Two

The History of Coffee

The historical path of coffee from its origin in Ethiopia to the Starbucks cafes that carpet the world's landscape is a long voyage of fact and fiction. Romantic and fanciful stories surround the discovery of the coffee bean and the mysteries that are still uncovered.

A Timeline of Coffee

600—While dates vary, from the years 600 to 850 A.D., most sources credit the discovery of coffee to an Abyssinian goatherd called Kaldi, who notices his goats prancing and cavorting after eating the berries from a nearby bush. Seeing the increased feistiness of the goats, Kaldi, allegedly, tastes the berry himself and appreciates the jolt of energy – without in any way being able to foresee the phenomenal global trend he is starting.

However regardless of how coffee was actually discovered, it remains undisputed that the plant was born in Africa, in the Ethiopian region of Kaffa. From there the use of coffee spread to Yemen, Arabia, Egypt, and Turkey.

1000—Avicenna, an Iranian physician and philosopher, makes note of the medicinal qualities of coffee, by saying: "It fortifies the members, cleans the skin, dries up the humidity that are under it, and gives an excellent smell to all the body."

1200—The first known cultivation of coffee occurs at Harrar, an Arabian colony, and travels quickly to Mecca. While at first used only as a medicinal beverage, coffee soon grows to be widespread as the beverage of choice throughout the Islamic world, largely because alcohol is prohibited. Transportation of the plant out of the Muslim nations is forbidden by the governments. The further dissemination of coffee began illegally.

1400—The first country to export coffee commercially, Yemen becomes the world's leader in the cultivation of coffee, a position it is to hold for the next three centuries.

1475—The first coffeehouse opens in Constantinople, setting the precedent for a male gathering place and a setting for intellectual exchange, political discussion, and business transactions. Coffee becomes so important to the Turkish Empire that if a man does not provide enough coffee for his wife, she is entitled to file for a divorce.

1500—Originally coffee beans were dried and chewed, sometimes mixed with fat and eaten, or fermented for a kind of wine, and only around 1500 coffee beans begin to be roasted, blended with spices, ground, and mixed with hot water.

1536—Turkish Ottomans capture Yemen, and with the capture, the coffee industry commences. The Turks spread coffee to the rest of the world.

1600—Willing to risk his life, an Indian pilgrim named Baba Budon smuggles several coffee beans out of the tightly controlled Yemeni monopoly. By taping the coffee beans to his stomach, he succeeds in bringing coffee to India, planting his bounty near Chikmagalgure where his original crop is the stock from which one-third of India's coffee is produced.

1607—Coffee is thought to have arrived in North America when Capt. John Smith founds the colony of Virginia in Jamestown.

1615—Coffee appears in Venice and begins to spread northward for the next 100 years. Street vendors add coffee to their standard wares, which include lemonade and chocolate.

1617—Church members in Venice protest coffee and its growing importance because they believe it is the drink of the infidels. The controversy is taken to Pope Clement VIII who tastes coffee and immediately christens it as the "true Christian drink."

1645—The first coffeehouse opens in Venice, Italy, and the spread of coffeehouses begins throughout Europe.

1650—The first coffeehouse opens in Oxford, England.

1652—The first coffeehouse opens London. Later, coffeehouses in London often grow into large businesses. Some firms that develop from original coffeehouses include Lloyds of London, the English stock exchange, as well as banks, brokerage firms, and trading companies.

1659—Coffeehouses continue to appear in the world's largest cities. In 1659, a coffeehouse opens in Marseilles, France, then, in 1663, the first coffeehouse opens in Amsterdam, and then, in 1673, in Paris. Known for their egalitarian codes where all types of men come together in a common place and no man has to give up a seat to nobles, coffeehouses are thought to be hot seats for political upheaval.

1668—Coffee replaces beer as New York City's favorite breakfast drink. Coffeehouses open in New York, Boston, Baltimore, Philadelphia, and other major cities. Most of these coffeehouses are more like pubs and taverns than the genuine coffeehouses of Europe because they also serve beers, wines, and ales. They also provide lodgings for sailors and travelers. One famous coffeehouse is the Green Dragon in Boston. At first, it is popular among British officers, but then, it becomes a hangout for the likes of John Adams, Paul Revere, and other revolutionaries plotting against England.

1675—King Charles II attempts to close coffeehouses because of the possibility of political unrest and because he believes his men are neglecting their families in favor of frequenting coffeehouses. The King rescinds his ruling because coffee drinkers are so incensed that they threaten to revolt and overthrow the monarchy.

1683—Coffee becomes popular in Austria. The Austrians make their own contribution to the history of coffee by using honey and cream to sweeten the strong beverage and thus creating the forerunner of cafe latte and laying the foundation for the cultural division between countries that drink their coffee black and ones that drink their coffee with milk and sugar.

1690—The Dutch steal live coffee plants from Mocha, an Arab port. From there, the coffee trees are transported to their colony, Java (modern Indonesia), beginning a long history of cultivation, production, and export.

1700—Yemen's three-century-old dominance in the cultivation and production of coffee comes to the end as Sante Domingue (modern-day Haiti) briefly holds the top spot. Haiti's coffee industry flourishes because of the island's rich soil and the existing slave labor force, which had originally picked sugarcane.

1705—France pioneers the first primitive filtration device for coffee. The grounds are placed in a securely tied cloth, typically of muslin or tightly woven burlap, and boiling water is poured over the pouch.

1713—A shoot of the coffee plant, stolen by the Dutch from Mocha more than a decade earlier, is presented to King Louis XIV of France.

1720—A French officer named Gabriel-Mathieu de Clieu, with the help of a lady of the court, breaks into the Royal Garden, steals coffee plants, and sets sail for the colony of Martinique where the prize is cultivated. The coffee then spreads throughout the New World.

1763—Venice numbers more than 218 coffee shops. Some coffee temples with old and picturesque atmospheres are still open today. Turin, Genoa, Milan, Florence, Rome, and Naples adopt the Venetian habit. Served in elegant shops or on rough common tables, coffee appears everywhere. Customers chat and gossip and men of culture begin referring to coffee as an intellectual beverage. The coffee tradition is still intact today.

1773—Coffee begins to be the favored drink in the American colonies after a revolt against a tax on tea imposed by King George. The cargoes of tea were chucked into the Boston Harbor. The event became known as the "Boston Tea Party" and patriots in Boston and elsewhere in the New World begin to change their allegiance from tea to coffee.

1800s—Because of a revolution in Haiti, many coffee planters lose their lives. Due to changes in the slave system and overall economics, Haiti loses its dominance in the coffee industry to Brazil, which becomes the leading coffee producer.

1819—A Frenchman named Laurens develops a method whereby hot water rises into a vessel and infuses the coffee. This is the first percolator, a device similar to one that becomes wildly popular in America during the 1860s.

1822—The first crude espresso machine is developed in France, but more than three-quarters of a century later the machine is patented by two Italians.

1864—Until Jabez Burns comes along, Americans remain far behind the rest of the world in coffee consumption and production. However, when Burns creates a machine that would effectively roast coffee beans, the majority of Americans take up the coffee habit.

1890—A young German doctor, Ludwig Roselius, invents a method of decaffeination after sudden death of his father who was a coffee merchant and taster. Roselius believes that his father died from the excessive amounts of caffeine that he ingested. Roselius patents his process of decaffeination and establishes a business in Bremen, Germany. His product is called Sanka, a clever abbreviation of the French phrase "sans caffeine." In the early 1900s, his product spreads throughout Europe and reaches American soil.

The method of decaffeination is simple. The green coffee beans are merely heated with steam to raise their moisture level, and a chemical is used to extract the caffeine. The beans are then washed, steamed, dried, roasted, and ground for consumption. This process has been slightly refined over the years, but it remains much the same today, except for the chemicals that are used to extract the caffeine.

1901—A Chicago chemist, named Satori Kato, creates instant coffee, which requires only boiling water to make a hot beverage.

1902—Luigi Bezzera, after working on an earlier French design and patenting a water and steam machine that makes coffee quickly, sells his patent to Desidero Pavoni, and in 1906, at the International Fair in Milan, Italy, they introduce the forerunner of the modern espresso machine.

1908—A German housewife from Dresden, named Melitta Bentz, begins experimenting with ideas to prevent the bitter overbrewed taste of coffee. She uses blotter paper cut in circles, and the resulting filters and filter papers are patented in 1908.

1920—Federal law prohibits the sale of alcohol. Coffee sales continue to increase in America due to Prohibition.

1923—Decaffeinated coffee is introduced in the United States under the name Sanka.

1971—Starbucks begins its empire of 6,010 company-operated, 3,391 licensed stores in the U.S., 1,511 owned, and 2,256 licensed coffee bars in 38 countries worldwide, emphasizing its fresh-ground, whole-bean Italian-style espresso beverages.

Chapter Three

Coffee: The Omnipresent Elixir

From humble beginnings in Kaldi's goat fields to the flooding of the world by millions of contemporary cafes, coffee has come a long way. No other beverage on the face of the earth is consumed as widely as coffee, except water. It is an almost inescapable poison that taints our bodies from the womb until death.

According to the National Coffee Association of the United States currently, 54 percent of the U.S. adult population drinks coffee daily, representing millions of coffee drinkers. Each year, the United States consumes about one-third of all the coffee grown in the world. And although Sweden and Finland, for example, have more coffee consumers per capita, the U.S. far outstrips both countries in terms of imports and total consumption. However, coffee drinking is declining as the beverage of choice, which gives coffee producers a multitude of sleepless nights, even without the caffeine.

Coffee Use over Time

According to one study on the subject, coffee drinkers begin their careers at low levels. In the early stages, however, the mold is usually cast. Whereas a cup or two is the order of the day for many coffee-drinking novices, this is not the case for veterans. Their daily coffee consumption slowly, inexorably, creeps upward – without apparent notice. Thus, 17 percent of the coffee consumers in the U.S. drink 3 cups per day, 11 percent drink 4 cups per day, 7 percent drink 5 cups per day, and 16 percent drink 6 or more cups per day. Obviously, one cup per day does not satisfy them anymore.

Coffee consumption usually increases during the early adult years as yesterday's adolescents start to drink it regularly. Once they have started, their coffee consumption progresses, sometimes to exorbitant levels. Coffee drinkers who polish off three or four cups per day are not uncommon. And there are millions of coffee addicts who regularly drink anywhere from five to fifteen cups per day.

It is obvious that moderation is the exception, rather than the rule. More than one-half of the adult coffee-drinking population consumes coffee in amounts that, all medical authorities would agree, are harmful to health.

Coffee Consumption Is Declining

Coffee drinking in the U.S. has been slipping almost continuously for the past fifty years, an economic maelstrom that the coffee industry has been helpless to curtail, even after wallpapering the landscape with Starbucks cafes and like-styled coffee parlors. Consumers are becoming aware of what coffee is doing to their minds and bodies and are seeking health-promoting beverages. In recent years, people have begun to cut down on their coffee consumption, however, have not given it up completely. Millions of coffee consumers in the over-fifty age group drink one cup per day.

Who Is Most Likely to Become a Coffee Addict?

In a study by the former U.S. Department of Health, Education, & Welfare, a profile sheds light on what types of people are most likely to become coffee addicts. The study found that heavy coffee drinkers differ from those who drink little or no coffee in several criteria.

In general, men were more likely than women to report drinking coffee. Men were also more likely to report drinking more than five cups of coffee per day. Caucasians were more likely to be heavy coffee drinkers than those of other racial groups.

Heavy coffee drinkers are also likely to have higher incomes. Heavy coffee drinking is also related to family income. This result, however, may be linked to age, as middle-aged people are more likely to earn higher salaries.

In general, the well educated and the uneducated were less likely to drink five or more cups per day than those who have an average education. Two occupational groups – manager-administrators and craftsmen – tend to have higher percentages of heavy coffee drinkers among their ranks than other occupational groups.

Heavy coffee drinkers tend to be drug users. That is, people who are heavy coffee drinkers tend to use additional drugs: cigarettes, cigars, alcohol, and others. Obviously, the synergistic effect of such combinations can create more pleasure.

For example, one study found that smokers are nearly four times as likely to be heavy coffee drinkers as are those who have never smoked, and those who used to smoke are nearly twice as likely to be heavy coffee drinkers as are those who have never smoked.

Speaking of the preference of heavy coffee drinkers, it is interesting to note that as consumption of coffee increases, the use of decaffeinated coffee decreases. One government study found that whereas 70 percent of regular coffee consumers drink one cup per day, almost 82 percent of those who consume regular coffee drink six cups per day. Whereas only 11 percent of heavy coffee drinkers use decaffeinated coffee, about 23 percent of those who drink one cup per day consume decaffeinated coffee. This speaks volumes about caffeine's addictive nature. The more caffeine you consume, the more you want to – or have to – consume.

The Bottom Line

Coffee is decreasing as the number one preferred beverage in the United States. Coffee is the "bum" drink of the 1980s. Whereas nearly 80 percent of the population used to drink coffee, now only about 54 percent indulge in this unhealthy habit. These dwindling numbers show that we are becoming more and more aware about negative effects of coffee on the mind and body, and we longer want any kind of it, decaffeinated or otherwise. Coffee consumers are discovering in ever-increasing numbers that not only does coffee provide zero nutritional benefits, but also that it can lead to pain and discomfort.

They do not need doctors to discover this. The medical community, by the way, is providing a great disservice to the patient community by remaining silent on the coffee issue and, worse, by misinforming the public about the controversy.

More and more research is pointing an accusing finger at the role of coffee in the development of a growing number of ailments and diseases. Thousands of newspaper and magazine articles are adding their weight and credibility in opposition to this destructive beverage.

Coffee's victims are conducting their own informal research and quit the dangerous brew in record numbers. Their self-research and self-prescriptions improve their health and life. Let doctors, clinicians, and researchers haggle over the finer points of medical research. Coffee's victims know the cause of their problems. They know that coffee is dangerous to their health – and yours.

Chapter Four

The Chemistry of Coffee

Despite coffee's global popularity, there is a troubling lack of understanding among coffee consumers concerning the focal point of the controversy. Mention coffee consumption and its related health problems, and most people will instantly think of caffeine, as if this drug were entirely responsible for any and all ailments that coffee produces. However, research shows that coffee also causes poor health. Nobody has ever suggested that coffee is a healthy beverage. The ultimate issue is to be able to assess the level of damage that coffee can cause.

Coffee contains a number of harmful compounds. The physiological implications of a few of them have been determined. Coffee contains trigonelline, chlorogenic acid, and tannic acid, a yellowish astringent substance, which stains the tooth enamel (and is used in tanning leather). Non-volatile acids in coffee include caffeic and quinic acids, plus some others that have not yet even been identified. Coffee contains volatile ingredients such as acetic, propionic, butyric, and valeric acids. It also contains furfural, acetone (which is used as a nail polish remover), ketones, and a variety of other acidic carbonyl compounds.

Coffee also contains cadmium. The Environmental Protection Agency (EPA) considers cadmium as a possible human carcinogen, which may increase the risk of lung cancer. Cadmium may also cause bronchiolitis, emphysema, or kidney disease if its accumulation in the body is excessive.

These are the major chemical components that occur naturally in coffee. Other compounds are added, subtracted, and even converted during the roasting and brewing processes to further obscure coffee's true identity. Acrylamide, for example, a recently discovered carcinogen, is formed during the roasting process. In addition, coffee trees are showered with different kinds of pesticides.

Thus, scientists have not put a finger on exactly which components in coffee produce the pathologies that their studies reveal. All we can tell is that coffee is responsible for coffee drinkers' ailments. Caffeine produces one group of health problems while the oils, acids, and other coffee's compounds produce another group of maladies.

For example, virtually all of the studies on coffee consumption accuse caffeine of being the major saboteur of the central nervous system (CNS). This is not at all surprising because caffeine is known as a CNS stimulant. However, many of the studies on heart disease and cancer treat regular and decaffeinated coffees as equal threats. Their findings suggest that the pathologies are dose-related.

Thus, as a coffee drinker, you may be more prone to pancreatic cancer or heart disease regardless of whether you drink regular or decaffeinated coffee. The same is true for gastrointestinal disturbances, which appear to be caused by coffee-produced variations in acid secretion and are not necessarily related to caffeine consumption.

While decaffeinated coffee producers make a big deal about relieving CNS symptoms, such as sleeplessness and irritability, obviously, they will not publicly address other possible coffee-related pathologies, such as cancer, heart disease, and gastrointestinal malfunctions.

The implication for coffee consumers is quite clear: those who value a healthy mind and body will quit drinking coffee completely.

What Is Coffee?

The scientific name of the common coffee tree is coffea arabica. It originally grew wild in Ethiopia. It now is cultivated in Java, Sumatra, India, Arabia, Africa, Hawaii, Mexico, Central and South America, and the West Indies. However, more coffee is grown in Brazil and Columbia than in all coffee-growing countries combined.

Coffea arabica is a shrub with shiny, evergreen leaves. It is 14 to 20 feet high when fully grown, although coffee growers usually trim and prune the tree to 12 feet. The common variety grows best at altitudes from 2,000 to 6,000 feet. As the blossoms of the coffea arabica turn snowy white, the coffee berries gradually ripen from green to yellow to red, which does not usually occur until the tree is at least five years old.

There are more than 100 different kinds of coffee plants, but the only two – arabica and robusta – account for about 99 percent of the world's coffee production.

Coffee and Pesticides

Caffeine is one of the natural pesticides produced by plants for self-defense. But coffee trees are heavily sprayed with different kinds of pesticides – man-made ones – which are extremely toxic to wildlife and humans. Among the poisons commonly used on coffee crops are endosulfan, chlorpyrifos, triadimefon, and diazinon. These chemicals have been classified as possible human carcinogens. There are reported cases of death from endosulfan and chlorpyrifos poisoning.

Another toxic chemical is trichloroethylene, which is used not only as a pesticide on coffee plantations but also as a degreaser in the metal industry and as a solvent in the dry cleaning business. Trichloroethylene is related to plastic chemical vinyl chloride, which has been linked to liver cancer.

Some of these and other dangerous chemicals that are heavily used in the agriculture of coffee-growing countries are banned or strictly regulated in the U.S. and Europe. Yet because they remain legal in those countries that export coffee to America and Europe, these chemicals may have an effect on the health of coffee consumers. My personal doubts that agricultural chemicals penetrate to fruits and vegetables disappeared after I washed a papaya with baking soda – it had a salty taste.

The Roasting Process Affects the Coffee's Chemistry

Roasted coffee beans contain an array of acids that can be summarized in four different groups: aliphatic, chlorogenic, alicyclic carboxylic, and phenolic.

In recent years, obviously to increase sales, coffee has been promoted as an antioxidant because it contains chlorogenic acid. However, the quality of this antioxidant actually degrades significantly under the high temperature of roasting and thus decreases its value. Moreover, the many risks of excessive coffee consumption clearly outweigh any antioxidant benefits.

The role of antioxidants is to protect cells from the damaging effect of free radicals. However, the coffee-roasting process creates numerous toxic chemicals that do the opposite. Degraded during the roasting process, chlorogenic acid increases homocysteine levels in blood plasma, which heightens the risk of cardiovascular disease.

The roasting process converts some coffee compounds into toxic chemicals with mutagenic and carcinogenic properties. Acrylamide is a carcinogen that appears in coffee under the high temperature of roasting. (Acrylamide also appears in other cooked carbohydrates, such as bread, French fries, and cereals, which has raised the FDA's concerns about its cancer-causing risk.)

Trigonelline, an alkaloid coffee compound, converts into substances with mutagenic properties. According to researchers, polycyclic aromatic hydrocarbons, which are both mutagens and carcinogens, occur naturally in green coffee beans; however, their concentration increases during the roasting process. This is especially true of phenenthrene, pyrene, and fluoranthene. Higher roasting temperatures and longer roasting times increase hydrocarbon toxicity. Research has shown that approximately 35 percent of these toxins penetrate into the brew.[7]

More than 800 volatile aromatic compounds, 42 of them phenolic, occur during the roasting process as a result of thermal degradation of chlorogenic acid and lignin. The aroma of roasted coffee beans consists of phenols, alcohols, aldehydes, pyrroles, furan, hydrocarbons, and other chemicals. Chlorogenic acid also forms the lactone that adds bitterness.

Coffee Contains Rancid Oils

The oils in coffee oxidize under the high temperature of roasting and exposure to air and light and thus become rancid quickly. Rancid oils deplete the body of vitamins B and E, degenerate tissues, and speed up the aging process.

Although some fats are more resistant to oxidation than others, due to differences in their chemical structures, in general oils oxidize with exposure to light, air, and heat. Oxidized oils form free radicals, which damage cells and thus cause degenerative diseases and lead to premature aging. According to Dr. Andrew Weil, rancid oils can even damage DNA.

A Better Choice to Restore Energy

Coffee is commonly used as a brain stimulant that helps to release dopamine, which provides motivation, alertness, and emotional highs. However, excessive coffee intake leads to overstimulation and depletion of dopamine-producing brain cells, which results in your feeling dull, fatigued, and exhausted.

Dr. Cass Ingram, in his book *Natural Cures for Killer Germs,* explains that because coffee is a strong diuretic, it depletes the body of certain vitamins and minerals, such as B-9, C, calcium, magnesium, and potassium.[8]

Instead of drinking coffee that flushes important nutrients from the body and depletes the vulnerable dopamine neurons, the number of which decreases with age even without coffee's effect on the brain, it is better to drink protein shakes, which nourish dopamine neurons and help to improve energy. Protein is a better choice to restore energy than coffee because it is an excellent source of tyrosine, an amino acid that is essential for dopamine production.

Drinking Coffee Leads to Addiction

If you were to ask the average coffee drinker, "Are you addicted to coffee?" He or she would probably answer, "Absolutely not." This is the problem with drinking coffee. Many coffee addicts do not know that they are hooked. It often takes a lifestyle change or a major medical problem to convince them otherwise.

Medical authorities point to the reality that using drugs to alter consciousness is nothing new. People use drugs for thousands of years, and in this respect, coffee's ability to reduce lethargy, stimulate, and enliven is legendary. The only new development in drug use is the change in the user preferences. Youngsters prefer caffeine pills, highly caffeinated energy drinks, marijuana, and a variety of hallucinogenic drugs to alcohol. Older people have stuck with alcohol, coffee, and certain kinds of stimulating drugs.

But why coffee drinkers who consume a cup or two per day become addicts who drink five to fifteen or more cups per day? Here, science is virtually mute. It was obvious from one study that novice coffee drinkers must have liked the effect that coffee had on them. Much research suggests that all coffee drinkers start their addictive careers with a cup or two per day. All addicts start that way. Alcoholics begin with just one drink. Smokers take just one puff.

A New Trend

Some manufacturers successfully market their products by using illegal drug names. Meth coffee is one example of using this approach. According to their website, it seems that consumers would be better off addicted to the meth coffee than to the actual methamphetamine. Does this mean that this company is offering meth coffee as an alternative to methamphetamines? Are we to read between the lines and deduce that coffee is a drug?

Some officials make efforts to prohibit promotion of caffeine-containing products under illegal drug names. In reality, these companies are not promoting illicit drugs; however, they are unquestionably promoting coffee as a legal substitute. And this poses a new problem to be vigorously confronted.

Although coffee is an addictive substance that has such attributes as tolerance and withdrawal and works on dopamine levels, just as all illicit drugs do, our officials do not openly admit the analogy. If they did, wouldn't they also be compelled to admit that all our society as a whole is functioning under the influence of drugs? And if so, prohibit coffee use? Could you imagine what would happen to our drug-addicted society if nobody got their fix in the morning one day? It would be a global catastrophe beyond the imagination.

Some people depend on their drug of choice so deeply that they will seek to acquire it at any cost. At one time, back in 1989, the former Soviet Union experienced difficulties with cigarette production. So frantic smokers stopped the traffic in the center of Moscow and turned the cars upside down. Only foreign emergency cigarette shipments helped to stop the riots. Drug withdrawal can create desperate and dangerous people. Nonetheless, smokers do not consider cigarettes to be a drug.

As with tobacco, coffee will continue to maintain its legal non-drug status, and therefore, our society will never get off drugs. It is only a matter of drug preference: some prefer light legal stimulants, like coffee and cigarettes, while others choose heavy illegal drugs. However, the transit from one to the other may begin imperceptibly. At some point, as our tolerance to regular doses increases, all drugs lose their initial effectiveness, and therefore, we increase our dosage, try other drugs, or both, all the while chasing that first high.

The Addictive Hooks: Tolerance and Withdrawal

The role of tolerance is one of the principal progenitors of addiction. Tolerance is a simple phenomenon, which is characterized by the fact that, over time, it takes larger doses of a drug to obtain the effect that smaller doses once produced. This is the reason that coffee addicts drink at least five and up to twenty-five cups per day. Increased tolerance is the reason that smokers light up 20 or 30 times per day instead of five or 10. The same reason that alcoholics cannot control their drinking: small doses are simply not as effective anymore, and therefore, they have to drink larger and larger amounts. If addicts do not receive their drug of choice, they suffer from withdrawal symptoms.

One group of researchers has shown that abstinence from coffee increases anxiety and muscle tension, whereas coffee intake decreases these symptoms. The habit is perpetuated because of the daily need to avoid the anxiety, headaches, tension, and other withdrawal effects caused by coffee abstinence.

In all likelihood, these two addictive elements – tolerance and withdrawal – are the reasons that we have millions and millions of coffee addicts today. Increased tolerance levels push them to larger and larger doses; withdrawal does not allow them to skip a cup because coffee alleviates their painful symptoms. This is a vicious cycle that can and must be broken; the pain, sufferings, and diseases that this addiction causes are epidemic in proportion.

More Dangerous than Ever

It may be hard to believe, but as dangerous as coffee has always been, it is getting worse. The blame for this growing danger can be directed at your friendly coffee producer and his economic bottom line.

For centuries, coffee arabica, noted for its rich taste and hardy aroma, has been the most popular of all coffee beans. Other kinds of coffee beans were available, but they simply could not compare with arabica.

However, robusta, hardy little beans, a product largely of Africa, India, Latin America, and Indonesia, is changing the preferences of coffee producers. Robusta was introduced in the early 1900s, but its decidedly unpleasant taste relegated it to a poor second choice among coffee producers, but only for a while. More and more coffee producers became aware that what robusta lacked in taste, it made up for something much more important: a richer, healthier net income.

Robusta makes everybody happy (except consumers of coffee). The coffee growers love it because it is hardy, disease-resistant, and grows rapidly. Since robusta can be grown at lower altitudes, it is not very susceptible to frost damage, and when frost does occur, it fares better than arabica.

More importantly, robusta is easier to harvest, and its average yields are more than double a per-acre crop of arabica. Obviously, this is important to the producer because it is readily available and cheaper than arabica. Never mind that candid coffee experts have compared robusta coffee's taste to that of burned rubber and its aroma to that of mold. Robusta is cheaper, and therefore, the use of robusta in the mass-market coffee has been steadily increasing. The use of arabica has plummeted, and robusta is now the mainstay of gourmet coffee shops.

The significance of all this talk about robusta is that these new-wave beans have twice the amount of caffeine compared to arabica. Since robusta beans are blended into nearly all mass-market coffees, the dire effects caused by the coffee producers' greed for fatter profit margins are obvious. You get stuck holding a grab bag of medical bills and ills, the full extent of which may take years to manifest, and never realize the real cause of your health problems.

The purity of coffee – the ratio of debris like rotten beans and twigs to actual pure fresh beans –has also been declining to levels that affect the overall quality.

According to the U.S. rules, 495 defects (a shriveled bean equals one defect, a pebble equals two defects) per 300 grams of unprocessed coffee are allowed.

The Food and Drug Administration rules permit unripe beans, gravel, and other debris to comprise as much as 30 percent of a cup of coffee. Almost all coffee sold in the U.S. is made up of coffee that is either instant or preground, the two types that, in all probability, contain debris and rotten beans.

Even though the public is largely unaware of this wholesale adulteration, coffee consumption is declining. Consumers may not know exactly how the beans are processed, but they quit drinking coffee. The reasons become painfully clear: coffee causes too many health problems. The worst of them are in store for women.

Chapter Five

Why Women Should Avoid Coffee

Women suffer from coffee-related pathologies with greater frequency and to a greater extent than men do. This unequal burden is present for several reasons. As women generally weigh less than men, they are more profoundly affected by comparable amounts of coffee. Likewise because children weigh substantially less than adults, they are more greatly affected by similar amounts of coffee.

Research shows that more women than men complain about coffee-related illnesses and diseases. Moreover, women often report a greater degree of pain and suffering from these pathologies than men do. But most significantly, women report that they suffer from a greater number of ailments because many of the diseases associated with excessive coffee consumption are female-related. The single most salient fact is this: women suffer from a greater number of the more serious medical problems than men do because they are women. Women appear to quit drinking coffee in much greater numbers than men do because of the unequal burden they seek to disown.

One study of more than 200 participants who had quit drinking coffee showed that women quit twice as often than man do. Moreover, the variety of their complaints greatly exceeded those reported by males.

- Women suffered from withdrawal to a greater degree than men did.
- Women's withdrawal symptoms generally lasted longer than men's did.
- Women experienced more withdrawal symptoms than men did.

Coffee consumed by males and females takes the same physiological course: it is easily absorbed from the gastrointestinal tract and rapidly distributed to all tissues and organs in the body. Research has established that each tissue bears coffee in approximately the same proportion as the tissue's water content.

It is bad enough that coffee flows easily to all parts of the body. That it flows to vital tissues in the female body is a great deal worse, particularly for the female of childbearing age. The sinister effects of coffee begin even before a woman becomes pregnant and endure long after the child is born. Breastfeeding mothers should be aware that caffeine that they passed through breast milk could cause irritability and sleep disturbances in their infants. However, the most frightening evidence is that excessive coffee consumption can cause miscarriages, stillbirths, infant's death, and birth defects.

Coffee Increases the Risk of Spontaneous Abortion

If a woman who drinks coffee does get pregnant, her problems are just beginning. When a pregnant woman drinks coffee, her ovaries and the fetus are bathed in this liquid shortly after it is ingested. (In a man the testes are subjected to coffee, leading some researchers to believe that it causes male infertility.)

A woman trying to become pregnant should avoid coffee. In a study, by Allen Wilcox of the National Institute of Environmental Health Sciences, women who drank just one cup of regular coffee a day were half as likely to become pregnant.

Several epidemiological studies have found a positive association between coffee intake and spontaneous abortion. This phenomenon presents a clear and present danger to the unborn. One such study, which included nearly 3,000 pregnant women, found that drinking three or more cups of coffee daily was associated with an elevated risk of spontaneous abortion.[9,10] The association between coffee and miscarriage found in this study was stronger than that of smoking or alcohol.

In another research study, the results showed that while moderate coffee consumption was unlikely to raise the risk of spontaneous abortion, higher levels would. The study concluded that the greatest danger begins at levels of six cups of coffee per day, which are hardly uncommon levels.

Coffee and Stillbirth

A study, conducted at Aarhus University Hospital, Denmark, in which 18,478 coffee drinking pregnant women participated, was set up to determine the connection between coffee consumption during pregnancy and the risk of stillbirth or death in the first year of an infant's life.[11]

This study concluded that pregnant women who drank eight or more cups of coffee per day had an increased risk of stillbirth when compared with those who consumed no coffee. The study concluded that drinking coffee during pregnancy was associated with an increased risk of stillbirth, but not infant death.

The Danish National Birth Cohort conducted a similar study to ascertain whether there was a connection between coffee consumption during pregnancy and the risk of fetal death.[12] In this study, 88,482 pregnant women who drank coffee during gestation participated. The data regarding their pregnancy outcome, as provided by the National Hospital Discharge Register, showed 1,102 fetal deaths. The researchers determined that there was a connection between high levels of coffee consumption and the risk of fetal death, especially after 20 weeks of gestation.

Premature Delivery

There is ample evidence that regular consumption of coffee can result in a shortened gestational length and decreased fetal growth. Researchers at the University of California at Berkeley studied 7,895 live births in the San Joaquin Valley. The results of the study supported earlier investigations that found that "the more coffee is consumed during pregnancy, the greater the chance of premature labor." Consumption of regular coffee also affected fetal growth, whereas decaffeinated coffee did not.

Coffee and Birth Defects

Many studies over the years have tried to link caffeine consumption to birth defects. The best-known study was conducted by the FDA, under the direction of Dr. Thomas Collins. Although the research was conducted on rats, the occurrence of birth defects revealed much damning evidence against coffee.

The most common birth defect that the researchers noted was the improper formation or total absence of digits on the paws of their offspring. The research also found that delayed bone development occurred, particularly the breastbone, although this abnormality was thought not to be permanent. The fetal abnormalities occurred when the rats were given caffeine in amounts equivalent to human doses of as little as two cups and as many as twenty-four cups of coffee.

Keep in mind that millions of women drink five or more cups per day. There are thousands of pregnant women who drink at least nine cups per day.

When this report was released, many researchers and coffee experts stressed that there is no evidence linking coffee to birth defects in humans. Although the FDA's study was regarded as an excellent, wellcontrolled experiment, it said that, the findings only confirmed that caffeine causes birth defects in rats and provides no evidence of its effect on humans.

However, in a landmark case reported by the Center for Science in the Public Interest (CSPI) a Virginia Beach girl suffered birth defects identical to those seen in the FDA's study. The CSPI said that they "were almost certainly caused by the mother's heavy coffee consumption during pregnancy."

According to the CSPI, the mother drank 10 to 12 cups of coffee a day during pregnancy, although she avoided alcohol, tobacco, and over-the-counter medications that might have caused birth defects. "I never took as much as one aspirin during my pregnancy. I was so concerned that a drug might hurt the baby," the woman said during a Washington, D.C. press conference. She went on to say, "I hope my experience will benefit thousands of pregnant women who drink a lot of coffee. Even aside from my case and the animal studies, it just makes common sense to avoid caffeine along with all other unnecessary drugs during pregnancy. When the risk is as serious as a birth defect, we should certainly err on the side of caution."

Researchers from the University of Nancy, France, who studied the effects of caffeine in rodents concluded that it could have teratogenic effects (birth defect effects in unborn fetuses) only if it is consumed in very large doses.[13] Thus, a pregnant woman who weighs 60 kg (132 pounds) would have to drink approximately 10 to 14 cups of coffee at a time to reach the level of toxicity that could lead to teratogenic manifestations.

Cautionary alarms have also been sounded in the New York office of the March of Dimes Defects Foundation, which disseminated a fact sheet that counseled women to avoid excessive coffee consumption during pregnancy. By "excessive" the national health charity meant six or more cups per day. The publication was sent to March of Dimes chapters and medical science reporters throughout the United States.

But how big a problem are we talking about? Each year, about 150,000 babies in the U.S. are born with birth defects – approximately one baby every 3.5 minutes. According to the Center for Disease Control, more than 12,000 babies die annually due to birth defects, which are the leading cause of infant's mortality.

An additional 560,000 conceptions result in miscarriages, still-births, and infant's deaths, due to defective fetal development. Combine these figures with a high percentage of natural abortions that are malformed, and you have a problem of considerable importance. It is a problem that is critically important not just to pregnant women, but to all women and mankind.

Listen to Your Body

When your body hurts, it is trying to tell you something. And women's bodies often have something important to say during their cycles in life.

Many studies have shown that women often begin to vehemently dislike coffee when they approach their menstrual period or become pregnant. Because of some inexplicable hormonal changes, pregnant women begin to find the idea of drinking coffee completely unappetizing We have found no formal research to explain this phenomenon, but it cannot be left unnoticed.

Somehow, the bodies of pregnant women begin rejecting coffee, as if their bodies knew that coffee would present a serious threat to the unborn and sought to announce this to naive and unknowing mothers.

Pregnant women, and the rest of us, should be aware of these signs of danger. We should listen to our bodies. They tell us the truth: coffee is dangerous to our health.

Coffee and Fibrocystic Breast Tumors

Excessive coffee consumption raises the level of stress hormones that then affect reproductive hormones. In many cases, hormonal changes caused by excessive caffeine consumption affect the breasts. Breast lumps often disappear after women quit drinking coffee.

A number of studies have implicated excessive coffee consumption in the development of fibrocystic breast tumors. However, doctors and researchers are still waging a rhetorical war on whether that proposition is true.

Whom do you believe? Well, when it comes to breast tumors, the true believers are the victims of this potentially dangerous condition who have eliminated the problem by giving up their coffee habit.

A Tough Dilemma

Benign fibrocystic disease of the breast is a common clinical problem confronting many women. Physicians recognize the disease as a benign, self-limited process that usually, but not always, comes and goes around the menstrual period. However, the disease often becomes relatively stable, resulting in painful, firm, nodular breast tissue that can and easily does camouflage malignancy.

This condition can lead physicians to misdiagnose malignant tissues as benign. The condition itself is also associated with the higher incidence of cancerous tissues. If the lumps are malignant, they must be removed (a costly, painful, and often disfiguring operation) to prevent the spread of cancerous cells. Mammography has been helpful with early diagnosis of malignancy, but it also can, according to some researchers, be inaccurate. Thus, women with chronic fibrocystic conditions may neglect repeated mammography examinations because of the well-publicized risk of radiation-induced cancer.

Women are faced with a tough dilemma: repeated mammography may expose them to unwanted cancer risks; forgoing these examinations may unwisely allow a malignant condition to go undetected. Biopsies can be painful and expensive.

Thus, the role that coffee may play becomes extraordinarily important for women. The available research suggests that reduced coffee intake can diminish or eliminate fibrocystic breast disease.

In one of the pioneering studies on coffee and fibrocystic breast disease conducted by Dr. John P. Minton, a group of 47 women with clinical fibrocystic breast disease were instructed to cease all methyl-xanthine (caffeine) consumption. Of the 47 women, 20 actually stopped drinking coffee.

The average coffee consumption of these women was from four to nine cups per day. The study showed that 13 of the 20 women who quit experienced complete resolution of all palpable breast nodules within one to six months. However, only one of the twenty-seven women who continued to drink coffee experienced resolution of the disease.

Not only did the fibrocystic disease resolve in the majority of women who stopped drinking coffee, but also the need for diagnostic breast biopsies dropped by more than one-third. Those who did not quit drinking coffee were required to undergo breast biopsies because their tumors had not disappeared, whereas only seven out of the twenty women whose tumors did not disappear following coffee cessation required biopsies.

Long-term follow-ups on these women showed a continued resolution of breast disease symptoms, as long as coffee abstinence was continuously maintained. The breast disease returned, however, as soon as coffee consumption was resumed.

The study also concluded that smoking tended to slow or prevent resolution in some patients, and a complete resolution of the disease required a year or more in women ages 45 and older. As indicated earlier, coffee drinkers are also more likely to be smokers. The study also noted that other studies tended to support this hypothesis.

In a matched study in Utah, Mormons exhibited significantly lower incidences of most types of cancers, including breast cancer, than non-Mormons did. The Mormon's faith forbids coffee consumption. A similar study of Seventh Day Adventists, who hold a similar tenet, yielded similar results.

Other studies also have reported that coffee is linked to fibrocystic breast disease. In one study, a significant number of women quit drinking coffee because they believed that the fibrocystic breast disease they were experiencing was caused by their excessive coffee consumption.

In all instances, the disease disappeared or had been significantly reduced following coffee abstinence. Think of it: a complete 100 percent experienced remission. No more biopsies. No more nagging fears about malignancies. No more unnecessary risks, simply by pushing away the coffee cup.

However, the controversy over fibrocystic lumps and caffeine consumption is far from over. Dr. Darrow Haagensen, assistant professor of experimental surgery at Duke University, was among those who questioned the findings. Dr. Haagensen, according to the CSPI, claims that there are three distinctly different breast disorders that have all been classified as fibrocystic breast disease.

Fifty percent of all women experience cyclical problems, including both breast lumps and breast pain before menstruation. Many women also have "diffusely lumpy breasts" that do not diminish after menstruation and neither do the "discrete masses" associated with the third type of breast disease. Within this category of breast disorders are gross cystic disease, the most common benign breast lesion, afflicting seven percent of all women, and fibroadenoma, afflicting five percent of all women. Women with gross cystic disease, according to Dr. Haagensen, have a two to five times greater chance of developing breast cancer than women who have never had fibrocystic disease.

Another physician, Dr. Gordon Schwartz, professor of surgery at Jefferson Medical College in Philadelphia and medical director of the Breast Health Foundation, also criticized Dr. Minton for not distinguishing between the several types of breast disorders. Dr. Schwartz claims that cyclical breast lumps and pain are the only type of breast disorders, he believes, can be diminished by caffeine abstinence.

According to the CSPI, however, Dr. Minton claimed that his studies were performed on women with "persistent unrelenting breast lumps and pain," not associated with the hormonal changes accompanying menstruation. He noted that some women whom he treated had fluid-filled cysts, a manifestation of gross cystic disease.

The author's personal experience and informal research revealed much the same results as those of Dr. Minton's. When consumption of coffee was discontinued, the breast lumps disappeared – whether they were cyclical or not. And neither me nor other women could be convinced that our problems were associated with anything but coffee.

The late Rose Kushner (no relation to the author), former executive director of the Breast Cancer Advisory Center, once wrote that she believed that Dr. Minton's findings would reduce the number of biopsies. "Doctors take out every lump and bump, so they won't be hit with malpractice suits," she claimed. "With Minton's findings," she said, "doctors will often have an alternative to biopsy and thus both help to keep down health costs and save women from the trauma of having a breast biopsy." Dr. Minton's finding, according to Kushner, is valuable because of the physical relief it might bring. "There is no reason," she asserted, "for women to have excruciating pain."

The controversy among the experts continues. And all the while, the suffering multitudes will make their own decision and quit drinking coffee. Research that will affirm Dr. Minton's work may take years to finish, and the American Cancer Society vows that it will not inform the public about Dr. Minton's findings until other scientists have verified his results.

Although studies show that there is a connection between high levels of caffeine intake and breast cysts and pain, and many women do experience relief after they quit, researchers state that correlations are inconclusive. Caffeine abstinence may not be a cure for every woman, but it can often be beneficial.

Coffee, Calcium, and Osteoporosis

Coffee increases the level of acidity in the body. To neutralize the acids, the body needs calcium, which caffeine, a powerful diuretic, excretes from the body.

Coffee drinkers may suffer significant calcium loss because if the body does not have enough calcium to neutralize acids, it uses its own mineral reserves from the bone tissues. This weakens the bone structure and increases the risk of osteoporosis. Bone porosity is common especially among women over the age 50. Bone porosity can lead to fracture of the wrist, hip, or the bones of the spine.

Interstitial Cystitis and Coffee

Interstitial cystitis is one of the pelvic painful disorders. It is an acute inflammation of the bladder, which is caused by a bacterial infection. The symptoms of interstitial cystitis may include mild discomfort, pressure, tenderness, intense pain in the bladder and the surrounding pelvic area, and urgent and frequent need to urinate.

Limiting coffee consumption is helpful in managing interstitial cystitis because coffee's diuretic effect increases undesirable urgency and frequency of urination. Coffee also worsens the condition by suppressing the immune system, increasing the acidity of urine, and heightening production of stress hormones.

Researchers have found that although urinary incontinence is common among women, and it depends on age, race, and pregnancy-related factors, as well as urological and gastrointestinal tract issues, coffee also plays a role in frequently increased urination.

A study, conducted in New Zealand, found that high coffee intake, four or more cups per day, was associated with doubling the risk of urinary incontinence in women. The study included 131 women with a condition known as "unstable bladder" and 128 healthy females. The researchers found that those who consumed three to four cups of coffee per day were more likely to suffer from "unstable bladder" than those who consumed only one to two cups per day.[14]

Chapter Six

Coffee and the Central Nervous System

Coffee is the most widely consumed stimulant in the world and the most popular choice to deliver caffeine to our system. Some 75 percent of all caffeine taken by consumers comes from coffee.

More than one-half of the world's population drinks coffee daily. Decades of research have shown that coffee is inextricably linked to numerous maladies, but the evidence clearly manifests only in its effect on the central nervous system (CNS).

Typical of the anecdotal reports on coffee is the CNS disturbance found in the case of a 26-year-old administrative assistant at a Chicago insurance company. A heavy coffee drinker, she picked up this habit from her mother who, in turn, probably picked it up from her mother.

She told researchers that she drank, on average, about 12 cups of coffee per day at an office where her fellow employees drank "pot after pot after pot." Her job was fraught with pressure, a condition that her coffee drinking most assuredly aggravated.

She reported being constantly jittery, all hyped up. Moreover, she likened her behavior to being high on speed, a drug she had experimented with and dropped because she did not like its effects.

In addition, she suffered, at times, from a faulty memory and impaired mental abilities. At times, she said, she just could not think straight. It was just like I was moving really fast. I just can't describe it." Fortunately for this young woman, she ceased coffee consumption, and only then did she become fully aware of how damaging coffee had been to her central nervous system. She reported that the "funny buzzing" in her head disappeared, and for the first time in years, she was able to "think straight." Furthermore, she was finally able, she said, to "recognize my real self from my false self" "Believe me, it's a welcome change," she said.

The Effect on the Central Nervous System

It is not surprising that coffee can have this kind of negative effect. Thousands of studies have substantiated similar problems. Coffee is used principally as a stimulant. A dose of two cups of coffee increases vigilance and wakefulness. Coffee acts on the central nervous system by increasing heartbeat and respiration. While coffee reduces fatigue, it disrupts complex motor tasks.

No one knows how some diehard coffee addicts would behave if they were free from their caffeine dependence; think about this a minute. How would they function without their morning cup of coffee? What would happen to productivity levels if employees were not always feeding their habit (on the job, no less) and bringing their drug-related hang-ups to the factories and offices of the world?

How many business deals are lost and otherwise messed up because of the mind-bending effects of caffeine? How many car accidents might have been prevented if drivers had not abused coffee while on the road? How would a clear-headed populace behave?

A subject in one research study offered some feedback. She noted that when she eliminated coffee from her diet, to her amazement, her well-being improved in ways she had never thought possible. Her power of concentration was vastly improved. She was calm and collected. She got along well with her supervisors and co-workers. She noticed the changes. Her co-workers noticed them as well. And she wondered aloud about how much better the world's productivity would be if all caffeine addicts quit their habit.

Coffee and Productivity

There have been few studies that have researched the question of whether coffee impairs productivity or work performance. It could easily be suggested, however, that workers who suffer from caffeine addiction also turn into inferior work performances. Headaches, jitteriness, irritability, impaired concentration, mood swings, and a whole constellation of other symptoms of caffeine overdose can certainly drain productivity from business and industry.

Health and behavioral changes that can be caused by caffeine addiction do not occur in a vacuum. Workers who suffer from its effects suffer on the job as well as off the job. It is obvious that employees who do not feel well do not perform well.

Coffee and Academic Performance

While research on the subject of caffeine versus performance is limited, one study that parallels on-the-job productivity was conducted by researchers at the University of Oklahoma who discovered a surprising relationship between caffeine consumption and college grades.

The researchers, Drs. Kirby Gilliland and Dara Andress, conducted a study in which both male and female students were gathered in four groups with different levels of caffeine consumption. The differences in academic performances, according to Dr. Gilliland, were striking. The abstainers and low-level caffeine consumers had grade point averages of C+. The moderate and high-level caffeine consumers had C− averages.

Dr. Gilliland claimed that the study showed a strong positive correlation between caffeine consumption and success in academic performance. He also reported that those who consumed large doses of caffeine thought they suffered more deleterious effects from their caffeine intake than members of any other group did. They reported more psycho-physiological disorders.

Whether these results could be applied in any wholesale way to the performance of workers in business and industry is quite another matter; however, regarding the academic world, according to

Gilliland's study, the more coffee you consume, the more likely you are to

- perform poorly,
- suffer anxiety,
- become depressed, and
- incur psycho-physiological symptoms.

In the business arena, where success is so highly prized and coffee addiction is so prevalent, one might expect the same disorders – perhaps even more serious ones. Coffee can and does produce remarkable changes in the central nervous system – changes that will bode ill consequences for both the coffee addict and his employer.

Good Health Is Good Nutrition

It is news to no one that coffee can make you behave like the nervous nellies in the old Robert Young coffee commercials. Coffee has been doing this to people since Kaldi got his first fix in an Abyssinian pasture, according to a legend. We have known about coffee's adverse effects all along, but only in recent years has the pendulum begun to swing the other way, that is, against coffee.

What happened? Why coffee drinkers quit their elixir in numbers that create panic among coffee producers? Because coffee consumers are more informed of side effects now than they were years ago. We are becoming more serious about health and nutrition, as well as about a vast number of chemicals that are polluting our bodies.

We are beginning to understand that good health means good nutrition and clean environment. We are beginning to learn that life's pleasures do not have to include addictions to endless varieties of damaging drugs: tobacco, alcohol, narcotics, and caffeine.

Getting High on Coffee

When you take a swig of coffee, it passes through the gastrointestinal tract where it is easily absorbed by your body. It reaches peak plasma levels within 15 to 45 minutes and passes quickly into the central nervous system (CNS).

Once in the CNS, caffeine's first target is the cortex and the medulla. It also stimulates the medullary respiratory, vasomotor, and vagal centers. These are the systems that are responsible for important functions such as breathing, blood vessel deflation, and operation of the vagus nerve, which provides innervation to the larynx, lungs, heart, esophagus, and most of the abdominal organs.

How dramatically these nerve centers are affected depends largely on the amount of coffee. If you consume a little, the effect will be minimal If you consume a lot, coffee can cause serious damage to your health.

The Most Common Reason to Quit

The need to escape the mental havoc that caffeine causes is one the most compelling reasons that motivates coffee drinkers to quit. This is the most common reason reported by the majority of coffee drinkers who decided to quit.

The symptoms of central nervous system disorders have now been well documented. They include mood disturbance, sleep disruptions, and withdrawal symptoms. The most common anxiety manifestations of coffee overdose are frequent urination, jitteriness, tremulousness, agitation, irritability, muscle twitching (including eyelids), light-headedness, heavy breathing, rapid heartbeat, and impaired concentration. Not everyone experiences all of these symptoms, and not all coffee consumers experience them to the same strength. However, subjects in several studies voiced much the same litany of complaints: jitteriness, agitation, and irritability led the wave of commonly mentioned symptoms.

A secretary of a large restaurant chain reported that she quit drinking coffee just to find out how much of her energy was naturally her own and how much was created by her coffee consumption. "I found out that at least half of my energy came from coffee," she noted. "And I thought I had such a dynamic personality. It was the coffee."

She went on to report that coffee allowed her to physically overextend Had she listened to her body, she would have slowed down. However, the coffee disguised the "go slow" cues, and she found that she was making a wreck of herself. "I was constantly worn out," she said. The woman's observation suggests that coffee suppresses a natural mechanism that tries to alert our bodies to slow down.

A Theory Behind

A research team led by Dr. Solomon Snyder, director of neuroscience at Johns Hopkins University School of Medicine, pinpointed the method by which caffeine acts as a stimulant. Snyder said that the discovery might point the way to improved drugs. Snyder and his group of researchers theorized that caffeine might work by blocking the action of a compound called adenosine, which they already were investigating.

Adenosine is one of the building blocks of DNA and is involved in cellular energy. But its crucial function, according to Snyder, is its role as a neuromodulator that tends to suppress activity.

The researchers also studied close relatives of caffeine, including theophylline, which is found in tea, and concluded that the stimulating effect of each of these methylxanthines was proportional to its ability to block adenosine, the natural anti-activity chemical, Snyder said.[15]

Coffee and Your Sleep

One of the most common complaints among coffee drinkers is that coffee affects their sleep. This result has been known for thousands of years and is one of the reasons why many people drink coffee in the first place: to stay awake.

Coffee has a substantial effect on sleep, as we all know. Ingesting coffee 30 to 60 minutes before sleep will dramatically reduce your ability to fall asleep, and many coffee consumers report that even when they do slip into some good R.E.M., their sleep is fitful and minimally refreshing. The effect of caffeine is even more pronounced in older adults. Caffeine exacerbates sleep disorders, according to a study reported in the Journal of the *American Geriatrics Society.* [16]

Some coffee drinkers, however, claim that their sleep is as restful as ever, regardless of their caffeine consumption. And without statistical evidence, who can refute their testimony? While it is obvious that caffeine affects all of us in different ways, it is equally important to note that we often do not know how it affects our system and cannot evaluate its effects on us while we sleep.

Subjects in several studies concluded that coffee drinkers do not have the least idea of what a good night's rest is all about. In brainwave studies, researchers have found that caffeine impairs the quality of sleep during the first three hours. This coincides with the rate of metabolic elimination of caffeine by the liver.

Another researcher noted that coffee consumption not only substantially delays the onset of sleep, but also diminishes the quality of sleep. Significantly more body movement was noted in heavy coffee consumers, and the quality of their sleep was substantially diminished.

What Caffeine Consumers Do Not Know

One study proved how ignorant we might be about our sleep. The researchers studied sleep patterns of medical students and found that many of them claimed that coffee did not disturb their sleep even when objective observations confirmed that it did. The researchers said that this denial reinforces the impression that coffee drinkers simply do not attribute undesirable clinical symptoms to their coffee intake.[17]

This situation illuminates one of the insidious aspects of coffee addiction: we are often unaware of how it affects us. Studies often reveal that respondents report that after they quit drinking coffee, they experience improved energy levels attributable to better, more restful sleep. They describe a good night's rest as an immense pleasure.

Surprisingly, the students believed that they had been getting a good night's sleep before they quit drinking coffee. In short, coffee is ruining the sleep of millions of people, and they do not even know it.

Coffee and Melatonin

Melatonin is the primary hormone responsible for sleep. Its release is controlled by serotonin, one of the main neurotransmitters. Melatonin is essential for a good night's sleep and the proper function of the immune system. Lack of sleep or disrupted sleep patterns suppress the immune system's normal activity. The body becomes more susceptible to infections and illnesses. The release of melatonin can be affected by excessive coffee consumption.

A group of Israeli researchers from Tel-Aviv University, Meir Hospital, Sapir Medical Center, and the Sackler School of Medicine found that caffeine consumption decreases melatonin secretion and affects quality and quantity of sleep.[18]

In a double-blind study, six volunteers drank decaffeinated or regular coffee on one day, and alternate beverages seven days later. Their sleep patterns were identified by actigraphy. Then, the participants drank decaffeinated or regular coffee again, and their urine was collected every 3 hours for the determination of levels of 6-sulphoxy-melatonin (6-SMT), which is the main metabolite of melatonin in urine.

The researchers found that drinking regular versus decaffeinated coffee caused a decrease in the 6-SMT excretion throughout the night. Regular coffee affected the quality, quantity, and length of time it took to fall asleep.

Sleeplessness and Coffee

Doctors and researchers have long been aware of that a link exists between worrying and sleeplessness, but this relationship has not been fully explored until recently. A new study conducted by the Department of Clinical Psychology at the University of Bergen, Norway, was set up to determine how worry affects sleeplessness and whether caffeine consumption increases the extent of worrying.[19]

Ninety-six female students participated in the study. The subjects varied from high to low levels of worry, which was measured by the Penn State Worry Questionnaire. Some of the students were administered 300 mg of caffeine, while others received a placebo. Throughout the testing, the women measured their level of nocturnal worry through a Nighttime Thoughts Questionnaire, and their quality of sleep was assessed by objective and subjective sleep parameters.

The researchers found that coffee clearly increased both nocturnal worry and sleeplessness. The objective measures of sleep parameters also showed that nighttime worrying caused sleeplessness. These results provide evidence supporting conventional wisdom that worrying keeps us awake at night. Even more importantly, susceptibility to nighttime worrying and sleeplessness is increased by coffee intake.

Coffee Drinkers Feel Better After They Quit

Not only is caffeine secretly ruining the sleep of millions of addict, but is also intruding on their health in many other stealthy ways. "I didn't realize how lousy it was making me feel until I quit," a 37-year-old housewife told researchers. "I just can't believe it was doing such a heavy number on me," she said.

Another woman, who drank coffee for 25 years, reported that coffee made her jittery. She did not recognize it until she quit. "I know for me when I'm not drinking coffee, I have more energy. I sleep better. I wake up in the morning feeling better. And I'm not as nervous," said a 37-year-old saleswoman.

Another respondent said that he would frequently become depressed on weekends and could not figure out what was wrong. After he quit drinking coffee, his depression disappeared. He was depressed, he subsequently realized, because he drank less coffee on weekends.

A young secretary who drank up to eight cups of coffee per day reported that everyone remarked "how much calmer I was" after she had quit drinking coffee. Another heavy coffee drinker, a 25-year-old photographer who drank eight cups of coffee per day, said that she "certainly didn't know coffee was causing that much change in [her] personality."

A 42-year-old executive who drank eight cups of coffee per day for 20 years reported that his caffeine dependence was far more damaging than he would have admitted before he quit. "I found that coffee has much more of a lingering effect than I believed possible. Since I've quit, I'm almost evangelical about it. Coffee had probably been bothering me a lot longer than I realized."

Again and again, research reports significant CNS disturbances – upheavals about which the victims were totally unaware. Only after they quit drinking coffee did they realize the gravity of their addiction, and the level of their physiological disturbances.

Case in Point

Nurses who attend patients recovering after surgery, at Scottsdale, Arizona's Mayo Clinic, noticed a disturbing trend, according to a Tufts University Diet & Nutrition Letter.[20] Patients were complaining about severe headaches – despite administration of potent pain killers.

The problem, according to anesthesiologist Joseph Weber, M.D., was that these patients were suffering from caffeine withdrawal because they had not had their regular coffee intake. The solution provided: administer recovering patients who drink coffee a shot of IV caffeine or give them coffee to drink following surgery.

The Right Decision

The most critical danger of coffee addiction is CNS disturbance, which brings some patients to the brink of mental disaster, a frightening emergency that neither they nor their doctors are prepared to confront.

In a paper published by Dr. Greden, director of psychiatric research, at Walter Reed Army Medical Center in Washington D.C., he reported a case of a 27-year-old nurse who applied for an evaluation at the outpatient clinic because of lightheadedness, tremulousness, breathlessness, headaches, and irregular heartbeats, which occurred sporadically two or three times a day.

The symptoms, according to Dr. Greden, had developed gradually over a three-week period. She denied precipitating stresses. When the evaluating physician commented on her apparent anxiety, she admitted feeling apprehensive, but correlated it with the presence of palpitations, chest discomfort, and irregular heartbeats.

Thereafter, the woman underwent a battery of laboratory tests, a physical exam, and an electrocardiogram. The tests revealed nothing unusual, save premature ventricular contractions, a characteristic feature of anxiety reactions.

During her final session with the evaluating internist, the woman was given drugs for her heart and then referred to the psychiatric outpatient clinic for treatment that the internist said was an anxiety reaction. However, the woman was unmoved by the doctor's diagnosis. She was thinking about possible causes of her symptoms and, thus, decided to quit drinking coffee. Within 36 hours, virtually all of her symptoms disappeared, including her cardiovascular disturbance. She complained of fatigue for one week but then began to notice, like many other quitters, that she was truly awaked in the morning for the first time in years.

Later, she challenged her system by temporarily returning to her coffee habit, and her heart disturbances returned immediately, documented by another EKG. She quit again and a two-year follow-up revealed that her symptoms have never recurred.

Caffeinism and Misdiagnosis

Dr. Greden also reported other cases in which doctors failed to identify the symptoms that were caused by excessive coffee consumption and, instead, blamed the symptoms on anxiety neurosis.

A 37-year-old lieutenant colonel was referred from the medical clinic to a psychiatric outpatient facility because of a two-year history of chronic anxiety. After three complete medical workups (all negative) and months of taking prescribed medications to ease the condition, a psychiatrist finally delved into his coffee consumption and learned that the lieutenant colonel was drinking between eight and fourteen cups of coffee per day. The psychiatrist's prescription for him was easy: eliminate coffee consumption. He did, and that was the end of his anxiety.

In another similar case, a 34-year-old army personnel sergeant underwent three medical exams and batteries of tests, both physical and psychological. These expensive, time-consuming tests were completed; however, no one thought to ask him about his coffee consumption. When doctors discovered that he was drinking between ten and fifteen cups of coffee a day, they prescribed the simple elimination of coffee, not the addition of other drugs. He quit drinking coffee, and his medical problems disappeared.

Unfortunately, doctors often mistakenly identify the symptoms that are caused by excessive caffeine consumption as anxiety neurosis and consistently fail to take adequate medical histories that could help them to determine the cause of their patient's complaints. With the proper record taking, however, they would have been better equipped to evaluate whether a patient's complaint was caused by excessive caffeine consumption or some other condition.

This finding is supported by a study in Belfast, Northern Ireland. A 28-year-old patient under the care of a consulting psychiatrist complained of palpitations, anxiety attacks, cold sweats, shortness of breath, and at times, tingling in her extremities.

A comprehensive psychiatric examination convinced the doctor to look elsewhere for the cause of her symptoms. Aware of earlier studies, he inquired about her coffee consumption. After learning that she was drinking 20 cups of strong coffee each day, the doctor suggested to quit it completely. She did, and after ten days, her panic attacks disappeared. After three weeks, she no longer experienced anxiety.

The doctor's concluding remarks have universal application to doctors around the world. "At the present time," he said, "it is quite likely that some patients are receiving anxiolytic (tranquilizing) drugs which are not only useless for this (anxiety) condition, but also may unnecessarily prolong a curable condition." The doctor concluded, "One can learn of its existence by simply asking a few questions."

These cases would certainly suggest that physicians have neglected the role of adequate record taking. If patients are going to avoid a lot of unnecessary examinations, tests, pain, and expense, they have to be more candid about their coffee intake. Doctors have to start asking more questions, and patients have to start volunteering more information as well. This is not occurring often enough, to the detriment of patients, mostly because neither doctors nor patients are fully aware of the large variety of abnormalities that are caused by coffee addiction. The central nervous system is just one of the casualties in the Great War between coffee and our minds and bodies. A more deadly prognosis is waiting ahead.

Chapter Seven

Coffee and Heart Disease

Despite years of studies, the relationship between caffeine consumption and the risk of coronary heart disease remains controversial. At least one aspect of the controversy is that the researchers do not always track what anecdotal evidence reports. The following is an example from one of the anecdotal studies.

A 57-year-old coffee drinker, Charlotte, drank up to a dozen cups of coffee every morning for the past 40 years. As many other heavy coffee drinkers, she occasionally had minor disturbances: sleepless nights, nervousness, and the like. By and large, she suffered no pronounced health problems that she could identify as being caused by her coffee consumption. All that changed after her heart began to act strangely. In the middle of one of her morning coffee-drinking binges, her heart began to beat both faster and irregularly. At first, she was alarmed, but thought the condition would subside. It did not. Instead, it persisted all day long. By the next day, the fluttering heartbeat disappeared, but it mysteriously appeared at least once or twice a week.

Despite regular checkups, she reported that her doctor had never inquired about her coffee consumption. When her persistent heartbeat irregularities brought her to the doctor's doorstep again, she was hospitalized. Still, her personal physician did not ask the most important question.

During her hospital stay, however, a heart specialist inquired about her coffee consumption. When she confessed that she was drinking a dozen cups each day, she was immediately prohibited from drinking coffee and was given medication to stabilize her wayward heartbeat. After she quit drinking coffee, her heart irregularities disappeared.

The Heart Muscle Is Disturbed

Each year, Americans, for example, consume more than two billion pounds of coffee – an enormous gluttony that affects both their morbidity and their mortality. It disrupts many organs and systems in the body, not the least of which is the heart; although no one has yet proven that coffee consumption causes heart disease.

When coffee is taken into our system, it is absorbed easily from the gastrointestinal tract and quickly finds its way into the central nervous system. Within minutes, depending on the amount of coffee consumed, the heart muscle is disturbed. Coffee is a myocardial (heart muscle) stimulant; therefore, excessive coffee consumption can cause adverse cardiac irregularities.

Just two or three cups of coffee can increase blood pressure by as much as 14 percent. Cardiac muscles that are stimulated by caffeine increase the force of contractions, heart rate, and cardiac output. The result can either increase or decrease the heart rate. Coffee dilates the coronary, pulmonary, and general systemic blood vessels by causing relaxation of the smooth muscle in the vessel walls.

Let there be no question left in your mind: when you consume coffee, your heart often has to work harder. Since it does work harder, doctors have long thought that coffee may be related to heart disease.

The Studies Reveal . . .

Researchers reveal a variety of stories that contain enough information to sow the seeds of concern that beg you to quit drinking coffee. One of the studies demonstrated that heavy coffee consumption could be an important risk factor for primary cardiac arrest in non-smokers.[21]

In general, the study suggested that coffee intake might predispose an individual to cardiac arrest due to arrhythmia (irregular heartbeat). This is precisely the sort of danger signal that flared up in the above-mentioned case. The reason for this increased risk is given among non-smokers is that smoking alters the way caffeine is metabolized, perhaps increasing its elimination by 55 to 60 percent, according to the researchers.

An earlier study conducted at the University of Minnesota, Laboratory of Physiological Hygiene, had important news for coffee drinkers who already had heart disease, and even for those who did not.

In this study, 7,300 men, ages 35 to 57, participated. They all had healthy hearts at the time of the research. The participants were questioned about their sleep, alcohol, smoking, and caffeine habits.

The study reported that heavy coffee drinkers are more likely to develop what doctors call VPB (ventricular premature beat), an irregular off-rhythm heartbeat. VPB will not kill you if you are healthy or at least have a healthy heart. People with healthy hearts can get VPB. However, for patients with heart disease, the VPB has been linked to heart attacks and even death.

The crucial question is this: how many thousands or even millions of people with undisclosed heart problems are today drinking five, ten, or even fifteen cups of coffee per day? Can you declare with absolute certainty that your heart is perfectly healthy? Probably not, unless you have just had a complete physical examination. But most likely you, as well as many other coffee drinkers, have not. Thus, the disease may be lurking right behind your heart's walls.

Even those coffee drinkers who do not suffer from heart disease ought to be concerned about their coffee consumption and the way it affects their heart. A dietitian who drank coffee for 45 years told researchers that she began to suffer from palpitations. One of her friends suggested that she should quit coffee to relieve the problem. She did, and her palpitations disappeared.

Coffee drinkers who developed high blood pressure and its sometimes adverse complications ought to look at quitting drinking coffee as a way to reduce the risk of heart disease.

"I was troubled with high blood pressure, and my doctor advised me to quit coffee," said a middle-aged woman. After she quit drinking coffee, she reported, "My blood pressure is normal now, and I'm sure it had a lot to do with the coffee." The woman took no drugs to normalize her blood pressure.

A 60-year-old machinist reported that he had been hospitalized a few times due to palpitations. He found that his condition was related to his coffee consumption, regardless of whether he drank regular or decaffeinated coffee. He quit both, and his heart began functioning normally.

As nettlesome as these heart disturbances may be, their significance pales in comparison to the more dangerous cardiac abnormalities, including coronary heart disease.

Myocardial Infarction

For the past 20 years, a number of studies have been conducted, charting the risk factors of chronic degenerative heart disease. The results produced a mixed picture. One of the premier studies on heavy coffee consumption and myocardial infarction showed a definite link between the two, even the most avowed coffee lover might seek separation.

Myocardial infarction is the degeneration of the heart muscle tissue that results when the tissue's blood supply is restricted by clogged or blocked blood vessels. This particular study showed that the risk of developing myocardial infarction is approximately twice as high for heavy coffee drinkers as it is for people who drink no coffee at all.

Researchers Hershel Jick and Dennis Slone undertook two studies. The first study compared 276 myocardial infarction patients, from 8 hospitals, in the U.S., Canada, New Zealand, and Israel, with more than 1,000 control patients who had other diseases. The second study compared 440 patients, from 24 Boston hospitals, with more than 12,000 patients who had other diseases.

In each study, they found that patients who drank up to five cups of coffee daily ran an approximately 50 percent greater risk of developing myocardial infarction than those who drank no coffee. Patients who drank six or more cups daily ran a 110 percent higher risk.

Another study, in which 503 patients with cases of non-fatal myocardial infarctions participated, concluded that coffee may trigger myocardial infarction in those who consume a single cup per day, have sedentary lifestyle, and have three or more risk factors for coronary heart disease.[22]

Coffee May Increase the Risk

One more noteworthy finding of the Jick and Slone study is that the heavy tea drinkers did not run the same risks as heavy coffee drinkers did. In fact, then, caffeine was even exonerated from suspicion, just as caffeine was cleared of being associated with pancreatic cancer. Thus, you are just as likely to develop pancreatic cancer or myocardial infarction by drinking regular or decaffeinated coffee.

However, several other conditions can increase the risk of developing this type of heart disease. The increased risk was greatest for those patients who were already predisposed to heart disease by variables including diabetes, certain occupations, smoking, and age.

The source of the link between coffee drinking and myocardial infarction remains a mystery. For this reason, the results of these two researchers have been criticized. The two studies were criticized even more strongly because their conclusions were based on a retrospective study, in which the evidence was gathered from patients who already had the disease.

Some studies, however, found no link whatsoever between coffee consumption and heart disease. The most well known was the Framingham Heart Disease Epidemiology Study, which was conducted under the sponsorship of the National Institute of Health.

More than 5,100 adult residents of Framingham, Massachusetts, were monitored for nearly 20 years in an attempt to find any link between dietary, physiological, environmental, and personality traits and heart disease. That report claimed to find no link whatsoever.

Other studies have found that coffee drinking is related to an increased risk of heart disease only when the coffee habit exists in conjunction with another dangerous habit—smoking. A study in Evans County, Georgia, found no association with coffee consumption, even though that section of the U.S. has been called a "stroke belt" because of its high incidence of stroke victims.

A study conducted in Finland reported an appreciable effect by heavy coffee consumption on the prevalence of myocardial infarction and coronary heart disease death. Another study revealed evidence that excessive coffee consumption is associated with coronary mortality, even though small amounts were exonerated.[23]

Think Decaf Coffee Is Better? Think Again

Most people assume that drinking decaffeinated coffee poses no serious health risk. A study, sponsored by the U.S. National Institutes of Health, suggests that drinking decaffeinated coffee could lead to elevated harmful cholesterol levels, which increase one's risk of heart disease.[24] The results of this study showed that the group drinking decaffeinated coffee experienced an eighteen-percent increase in the fatty acids in their blood, which drive the production of LDL (bad) cholesterol.

Conclusions

Despite the wide-ranging and often conflicting results from the studies, a number of conclusions can be drawn from this and other data.

- Coffee has a profound effect on the heart and has been shown to cause palpitations, ventricular premature beats, extrasystoles (extra contractions between heartbeats), and abnormally fast and slow heartbeats.

- Coffee has been associated with both low and high blood pressure.
- Coffee – whether regular or decaffeinated – has been associated in some studies with myocardial infarction.
- People with a history of heart disease ought to avoid coffee because it can pose a significant hazard to their health and longevity.
- People who are predisposed to heart disease, those who are overweight, or smoke ought to avoid drinking coffee because they increase their risk of heart disease more than those who do not drink coffee. While further research is necessary to determine the reason why coffee may lead to heart disease, for the prudent, health conscious public there are already enough reasons to quit.
- Drinking a few extra cups of coffee each day can boost blood pressure, heart rate, and stress levels enough to increase a person's risk of developing heart disease more than moderate coffee consumption This warning comes from James Lane, associate research professor of psychiatry, Duke University, Durham, North Carolina.

In a study of habitual coffee drinkers, reported by the Society for Advancement of Education, Lane showed that the equivalent of four or five cups of coffee can raise blood pressure up to five points, compared to days when the subjects drank only one cup. Not only did the ill effects of coffee intake show up within an hour after consumption, but the subjects' blood pressure also remained elevated all day. The findings also showed that the subjects complained of higher levels of stress during the day and showed a corresponding increase in heart rate.

The Central Issue

The relevant message concerning this study is not that a five-point rise in blood pressure is excessive, because it is not. However, such an increase can have weighty clinical implications over time. The more coffee you consume during a day, the higher your blood pressure is likely to be. Over many years, said Lane, this increase may heighten your risk of suffering a heart attack or stroke, even though you may not have high blood pressure now.

Chapter Eight

Do You Have the Stomach for Coffee?

There is ample research that suggests coffee is causally linked to peptic ulcers. And even greater evidence demonstrates that once you have developed such an ulcer, coffee is the worst beverage you can drink.

Stomach ulcers are usually caused by bacteria and certain medications These are the main factors that cause damage the protective layers of the gut, allowing digestive juices to irritate the tissues. However, coffee is also a strong irritant because it stimulates acid secretion and, therefore, can aggravate an ulcer.

In one of the earliest studies on coffee consumption and peptic ulcers, a group of researchers tested the gastric secretory response of 36 patients with peptic ulcers and 50 subjects without ulcers. The results were dramatic. The researchers discovered that not only does coffee stimulate gastric secretion, but also that excessive consumption may contribute to the development of peptic ulcers in ulcer-prone people. Furthermore, those patients who develop peptic ulcers have a much more difficult time controlling the disease if they continue to drink coffee.

The researchers also learned that Sanka and other decaffeinated coffees stimulate the secretion of gastric acids. Decaffeinated coffee was found to be responsible for the painful and sometimes dangerous over-secretion of stomach acids. The researchers suggested that coffee stimulates gastric secretion because of its caffeine content and other agents, such as natural roasting by-products and irritant volatile oils. The report pointed out that coffee provokes a prolonged increase in the total output of acid by the stomach in patients with peptic ulcers. In view of all this, the report urged that people with peptic ulcers, or those who are predisposed to such ulcers, refrain from drinking coffee.

The study ended on a rather peculiar note suggestive of a kind of absurdity that is sometimes present in medical circles. "It is realized," the report stated, "that the psychological hardship of total abstinence is sometimes more aggravating to the ulcer patient than the pharmacodynamic effects of a contraindicated substance." In such in stances, the report concluded that "a single cup of coffee with sugar and milk or cream with a meal could be allowed."

Despite the Hippocratic Oath

We have learned that researchers tell us that there are coffee addicts who are so severely hooked on their drug that the psychological pain of not having their fix is greater than the real physical pain from peptic ulcers.

And these clinicians, in their wisdom, suggest that it is better to perpetuate the addiction than to forgo coffee and live a healthier life. Please explain to me the so-called wisdom in this medical advice.

Heartburn and Coffee

Heartburn is a burning sensation beneath the breastbone that happens when a spastic back-flow of acidic stomach contents flows into the esophagus. Millions of us experience it all the time. It is a frequent companion of a significant portion of heavy coffee drinkers, perhaps as many as 40 to 50 percent.

Presumably, this back-flow is caused by an increase or a decrease in lower esophageal sphincter pressure (LESP). Without getting into the technical jargon that doctors use, the sphincter is a muscle that opens and closes the port between the stomach and the esophagus.

The exact relationship between coffee and LESP is yet to be determined; however, the pain experienced, often accompanied by gas and diarrhea, is made worse by certain foods, and above all else – coffee. Studies have confirmed that heartburn is linked to excessive coffee consumption. And "excessive" can be any amount, depending on the individual. Some coffee drinkers report such distress after only a cup or two; others can consume five or ten cups of coffee a day before they begin to feel the symptoms.

In a study of the heartburn problem, Dr. Sidney Cohen tested 57 subjects who had reduced their coffee consumption because of gastrointestinal disorders. Most of the study subjects (65 percent) had reduced their coffee intake. Some 35 percent had quit entirely. Upon reintroducing coffee into their systems through tubes, it was found that almost 50 percent of them suffered from gas, including bloating, belching, and passage of flatus. Thirty-nine patients suffered from diarrhea; nine percent of the patients complained of chest pain; and about 11 percent reported nausea.

The study suggested that persons who experience coffee-induced stomach disorders have no way to avoid them unless they quit drinking coffee. "Since the heartburn symptoms can be modified by reduction in acid secretion alone," the report stated, "this goal may be sought in a decaffeinated coffee product. However, previous studies suggested that decaffeination does not achieve this goal since it alters acid secretion only minimally."

The concluding note to this study is that coffee may cause or aggravate heartburn, regardless of whether the coffee you drink is regular or decaffeinated. Another study reported that decaffeinated coffee has the potential to induce heartburn and acid reflux.

More Evidence

One more study reached the same conclusion, although it found that coffee lowers the sphincter pressure instead of increasing. In this report, volunteer subjects drank coffee and were later tested for heartburn symptoms. Again, the patients were found to have significantly increased their heartburn symptoms after drinking coffee, even though no one has, as yet, put a finger on precisely why this occurs.

Obviously, future research will need to determine the exact link between coffee consumption and gastrointestinal disorders. However, the knowledge that coffee – whether regular or decaffeinated – causes these disorders ought to be a sufficient reason to quit the habit now.

Some of the digestive and gastrointestinal disorders associated with regular coffee do not disappear when one switches to decaf. Researchers have also found that decaffeinated coffee affects mineral absorption, including iron, calcium, and magnesium.

Coffee Heightens the Risk of Digestive Disorders

Coffee addiction can lead to various other digestive disorders because the caffeine, oils, and acids in coffee cause overproduction of hydrochloric acid. Decaffeinated coffee also causes excessive stomach acid secretions because it contains the same oils and acids that are found in regular coffee and trace amounts of caffeine and methylene chloride, the chemical used to decaffeinate the beans. Therefore, whether regular or decaffeinated, coffee increases the risk of developing stomach ulcers and other digestive ailments.

In one study, 25,000 coffee drinkers showed an approximately 72 percent higher risk of developing stomach ulcers than those who did not drink coffee. Drinking coffee, even in small amounts, also exacerbates already existing digestive disorders. The daily irritation can cause further damage, disease progress, inflammation, and pain.

Stomach Disorders Develop Over Time

The Adrenal Foundation conducted a survey to determine the effect of coffee on the stomach. Most of the participants drank somewhere around eight cups of coffee a day, more than the average coffee drinker consumes. Some coffee drinkers began complaining about the effects of coffee after as little as one cup per day; others did not start complaining or to quit until they had reached higher levels – ten to fifteen cups per day.

It was noted that those participants who quit primarily because coffee was extremely distressful to their gastrointestinal systems drank little more than anyone else in this survey, which is eight cups per day. However there were people who suffered from ulcers and stomach cramps and drank as few as three to five cups per day, and there were many who drank upwards of 20 cups per day.

Since the average coffee consumption is around three to four cups per day, obviously coffee drinkers are begging for stomach problems, now and in the future. Moreover, those who drink three cups per day today may begin to drink five cups a day tomorrow. Today's experimenters are tomorrow's addicts.

Perhaps more importantly than the amount of coffee you drink each day is the length of time you have been excessively drinking coffee. While disturbances of the heart, lungs, and central nervous system seem to be fairly evenly distributed throughout the group of participants, regardless of their age, stomach disorders were not. The gastrointestinal problems appeared more likely to occur among those participants who have been drinking excessive amounts of coffee for much longer periods of time. The risk of severe stomach disorders seemed to increase in direct proportion to the number of years the respondents drank coffee.

A doctor included in this survey have suggested that because the oils and acids in coffee irritate the stomach lining's tissues, which are continually assaulted by these chemicals, the tissues, over time, would become inflamed and painful. While for most coffee drinkers it takes many years to develop this inflammation, excessive coffee consumption over many years will, predictably, lead to this result.

Thus, if there were any predictive value in coffee addiction statistics, it would clearly suggest that at least 30 million American coffee drinkers who have been drinking five cups of coffee per day will develop serious stomach problems through their coffee drinking habit. The prognosis is substantially poorer for the 21 million Americans who drink six or more cups per day. Nearly 50 percent of coffee drinkers can develop serious stomach problems. This is a bad prognosis, at best, and a terrifying one, at worst.

Chapter Nine

Coffee and Cancer

The most frightening of all possible prognoses of coffee addiction is cancer. Does coffee cause cancer? The results over the years have been contradictory. The jury is still out. More than one-half of the population that is over the age of ten drinks coffee. The average per capita rate is two cups per day. The average coffee drinker in the U.S. consumes three to four cups per day. Nearly 30 million coffee drinkers in America polish off five to 25 cups per day. One can imagine the shock value of announcing that coffee causes cancer.

The cancer scare began in earnest back in the 1980s when a group of Harvard researchers studied the effects of coffee drinking on 369 hospital patients and reached this conclusion: there is an 80 percent higher risk of pancreatic cancer associated with drinking two cups of coffee daily. If this is true, some 75 million coffee drinkers may expose themselves to pain, suffering, and possibly premature death due to pancreatic cancer. This is the risk at lower levels of coffee consumption The potential gets markedly higher for heavy coffee drinkers.

Number of Cups Daily	Increased Risk
1-2	2.1 times
2	2.7 times
3-4	2.8 times
5 or more	3.2 times

When you combine the figures on coffee consumption provided by the American National Coffee Association and the Harvard research group, the average U.S. coffee drinker consumes coffee at a rate that nearly triples the risk of pancreatic cancer. If realized, this outcome would be catastrophic. In fact, it was so overwhelming to some coffee drinkers that the cancer scare was the most important precipitating reason to quit. In one survey, ten percent of those who quit drinking coffee said that "fear of cancer" was what motivated them to quit.

What Is the Pancreas?

The pancreas is one of the body's most vital organs. It is situated just behind the stomach. The seven-inch-long fish-shaped organ secretes digestive enzymes into the small intestine, which help the body turn food into energy.

Chances of Survival Are Slim

Cancer of the pancreas has the highest fatality rate of all types of cancer. Only about three percent of those who develop pancreatic cancer live three years after being diagnosed and only two percent after five years.

The American Cancer Society provided the following current somber statistics regarding cancer.

Cancer	Cases	Deaths
Lung	174,470	162,460
Colon/Rectum	148,620	55,170
Breast	213,920	41,430
Prostate	234,460	27,350
Pancreas	33,730	32,300

Pancreatic cancer is the fifth most common type of cancer in the U.S. Although pancreatic cancer is not the most prevalent of all forms of cancer, it is certainly one of the deadliest. The number of cases is gradually climbing each year. It strikes men slightly more often than women. But worst of all, if you are stricken with pancreatic cancer, you are likely to die from it – and soon.

The link between coffee consumption and pancreatic cancer should not be taken lightly, even though large numbers of coffee consumers are likely to do so. Disbelief has always been a great hindrance to behavior modifications, and it is only to be expected that coffee consumption and cancer statistics would be no different.

The Harvard Study

The Harvard Study involved 1,013 patients in 11 large hospitals in Boston and Rhode Island. The data was obtained on the smoking and drinking habits of the 369 patients with diagnosed pancreatic cancer and 644 patients who were hospitalized with other diseases. The results were unexpected.

The researchers set out to see if there was a link between pancreatic cancer and tobacco or alcohol use, however, they found that the consumption of alcoholic beverages did not significantly relate to any increase in pancreatic cancer. They also drew a blank on the association between increased cancer risk and the use of tea, pipe tobacco, or cigars. However, the data showed "a consistent association of pancreatic cancer with coffee consumption within each category of smoking; and the data for all smokers and nonsmokers showed a consistent trend with coffee consumption after adjustment for smoking."

The findings of the Harvard group are consistent with the previous investigations that also showed an association between coffee consumption and pancreatic cancer. In another case-controlled study in which 94 patients participated, researchers found that patients with pancreatic adenocarcinoma tended to drink more decaffeinated coffee than in the control group.

Coffee or Caffeine?

The Harvard study not only pointed an accusatory finger at regular coffee, but also on decaffeinated coffee because the researchers failed to find any link between pancreatic cancer and tea consumption. Presumably, such a finding would rule out any link between caffeine and pancreatic cancer because tea also contains caffeine. Thus, it appears that whether you drink decaffeinated or regular coffee, you still share an increased risk of pancreatic cancer, according to the researchers.

The Harvard researchers disagreed somewhat with the earlier findings regarding decaffeinated coffee reported by a group of Maryland researchers. In that study, it was found that habitual consumption of decaffeinated coffee was significantly greater among pancreatic cancer patients than in controls. The study also noted that the chemical tricholororethylene (TCE), once widely used to decaffeinate coffee, is the same chemical that was formerly used to dry-clean clothes. The Maryland researchers found that men in the dry cleaning business had an increased risk of pancreatic cancer.

However, the Harvard researchers believed that "in view of the relatively recent use of decaffeinated coffee on a large scale, it seems unlikely that this particular kind of beverage has a causal relationship with pancreatic cancer appearing at present. It seems more likely that the high consumption of decaffeinated coffee is a reflection of generally high coffee consumption by these patients in the past."

The TCE Cancer Scare

TCE was the most widely used chemical until the 1970s when the National Cancer Institute reported that TCE caused liver cancer in laboratory mice. That memorandum sent coffee makers scampering for safer chemicals. Companies stopped using TCE in July of 1975, but no formal action has been taken to ban TCE from foods, drugs, and other products. The FDA, obviously, is awaiting further information on the safety of this chemical. However, the FDA has ruled that the residue of methylene chloride, the chemical now used to decaffeinate beans, must not exceed ten parts per million. Dr. Brian MacMahon, who led the Harvard research group, said that the association between coffee drinking and pancreatic cancer ought to be evaluated with other data. Dr. MacMahon said: "If it (the association) reflects a causal relation between coffee drinking and pancreatic cancer, coffee use might account for a substantial portion of the cases of this disease."

"If the distribution of coffee consumption in our control group reflects that in the general population ... we estimate the proportion of pancreatic cancer that is potentially attributable to coffee consumption to be slightly more than 50 percent." In short, Dr. MacMahon suggested that if the link between excessive coffee consumption and pancreatic cancer is a valid one, then at least 10,000 lives might be saved each year if the victims do not drink coffee. Dr. MacMahon, who used to drink three cups per day believes in what he says; when the results became known, he quit drinking coffee.

For the past 20 years about 18 controlled studies have suggested the possibility that excessive coffee consumption could be associated with pancreatic cancer, although the evidence is mixed. Since the results are inconclusive and more research is needed, it is up to coffee consumers to decide whether to take the risk.

Coffee and Lung Cancer in Smokers

A study conducted at the Department of Epidemiology, Roswell Park Cancer Institute in Buffalo, New York, involved 993 current and former smokers with diagnosed lung cancer and 986 hospital controls smokers with other conditions.[25]

The study found an association between high levels of coffee intake and an elevated risk of lung cancer for current and former smokers. Two cups of black tea per day were not a factor for lung cancer risk; however, it was for those participants who drank two to four cups of coffee per day. Decaffeinated coffee showed a decreased risk for both participant groups who consumed one to two cups daily.

Coffee Poisons the Liver

Your liver has to deal with a tremendous amount of toxins daily. It detoxifies most of the poisons received with air and from food. However, there are chemicals that poison the liver. And, in this respect, coffee should not be taking lightly. Coffee contains toxic chemicals among which are polycyclic aromatic hydrocarbons (PAH) and tannic acid.

Both PAH and tannic acid have been suspected of causing liver cancer.[26]

Coffee and Bladder Cancer

Other forms of cancer may also be linked to excessive coffee consumption, particularly cancer of the urinary bladder. Cancer of the bladder has long been recognized as a hazard of environmental exposure to certain chemicals. Likewise, smoking increases the risk of developing this cancer, particularly in male smokers. However, a significant number of bladder cancer cases remained unexplained by tobacco use or exposure to chemicals. There is a possibility that this form of cancer may be linked to excessive coffee consumption.

Bladder cancer is the sixth most frequently occurring type of cancer in the U.S. According to the American Cancer Society, bladder cancer affects more men than women, mostly older adults. Men have a one in twenty six chance of developing this type of cancer; for women it's one in eighty four.

The main risk factors for bladder cancer are believed to be smoking, exposure to certain highly toxic chemicals, and parasite infestation However, 34 controlled and 3 cohort studies showed that excessive consumption of coffee also increases the risk, which appears to start at five cups and increases accordingly. Those who consume ten cups of coffee per day have an 80 percent higher chance of developing the disease than those who consume less.

Since men are more prone to developing bladder cancer than women, more than four cups of coffee per day could be sufficient to heighten their risk. In one study, published in the Canadian journal *Chronic Diseases,* 549 men with bladder cancer and 1, 099 men in a control group participated. Men who drank four cups of coffee or more daily doubled their risk of developing bladder cancer, compared to the participants of the control group who did not drink coffee.[27] The researchers concluded that approximately 33 percent of bladder cancer cases in men could be prevented if they did not consume excessive amounts of coffee. In Canada, bladder cancer is the fourth most common form of cancer in the male population.

According to the researchers, excessive consumption of coffee presents a higher risk of developing bladder cancer than exposure to toxic industrial chemicals, such as asbestos, but is less dangerous than smoking.

In another Canadian population-based, case-control study, 480 pairs of male patients, 152 pairs of female patients, and controls were interviewed regarding their use of cigarettes, coffee, non-public water supplies, and their exposure to certain industrial chemicals. These patients had newly diagnosed cases of bladder cancer.

The study revealed that coffee was the beverage associated with an increased risk of bladder cancer. The increased risk among men was about 1.5 times higher for regular and instant coffee drinkers and about 1.4 times higher for all kinds of coffee. The relationship with other beverages was not statistically significant.

The following is a rundown of the increased risk of bladder cancer that these Canadian researchers discovered:

Two cups per day—1.2 times
Three to four cups—1.3 times
More than five cups—1.5 times

Strangely enough, instant coffee was proven even more dangerous than regular. As a whole, the increased risk of bladder cancer was not dose-related. That is, drinking more coffee did not materially increase the chances of developing the cancer.

The findings parallel several other studies on coffee consumption and bladder cancer that suggested coffee's association with the disease. However, the dose required to significantly alter the statistics has not yet been determined. Further research will, no doubt, shed more light on how excessive coffee consumption is related to bladder cancer as well as all other types of cancer.[28,29,30]

Coffee and Estrogen

Coffee stimulates the adrenal glands and forces them to overproduce stress hormones, which may lead to hormonal imbalance. For women, hormonal imbalance can be a serious concern. Chronically excessive caffeine consumption can affect the level of estrogen. Heightened levels of estrogen are associated with the risk of developing certain types of breast cancer.

Coffee and Non-Hormone-Related Breast Cancer

A study conducted by a group of researchers from Harvard University and their Japanese colleagues found that women consuming four or more cups of coffee per day (or equal or higher amount of caffeine from other sources) significantly increased their risk of developing the non-hormone-related types of breast cancer – estrogen-receptor-negative and progesterone-receptor-negative. The study also showed a development of tumors larger than two centimeters (one inch is equal to 2,5 centimeters) and revealed a risk of developing breast cancer in women with benign disease who consume high doses of caffeine daily.[31]

The researchers disclosed 1,188 invasive breast cancer cases during a ten-year follow-up study of 38,432 women, ages 45 and older, who excessively consumed caffeine. The study concluded that the higher the level of caffeine intake, the higher the risk of developing the non-hormone-related types of breast cancer.

According to the researchers, there are different subtypes of breast cancer with different risk factors, which might not be taken to the consideration in the previous studies that found no association or weak connection between caffeine and breast cancer. The study concluded that high level of caffeine intake does not affect the development of estrogen-related tumors, however, there is a risk of developing hormone-receptornegative breast cancer.

Toxic Mold in Coffee

Green coffee beans may contain mycotoxin Ochratoxin-A, which is formed by the mold fungi Aspergillius and Penicillium. This toxin commonly grows on stored crops, such as wheat, rye, barley, oats, rice, nuts, dried fruits, spices, and coffee.

Ochratoxin-A has been recognized by the World Health Organization (WHO) as a potential carcinogen, immuno-suppressant, and nephrotoxic, embryotoxic, and teratogenic agent, both in humans and animals. Based on studies, the International Agency for Research on Cancer (IARC) has classified Ochratoxin-A as a "possible human carcinogen."

Scientists have not yet been able to conclude whether Ochratoxin-A causes cancer in humans; however, it does cause mammary gland (breast) cancer in female rats and kidney tumors in both genders.[32] Not every chemical that causes cancer in animals has the same effect in humans; however, those carcinogens that do cause cancer in humans also produce tumors in laboratory animals.

Ochratoxin-A is a very stable toxic chemical that cannot be easily destroyed during the roasting process and, therefore, penetrates into the brew. Studies have shown that it appears in the blood, tissues, and even breast milk. Ochratoxin-A affects the kidneys, causing a disease called Balkan Endemic Nephropathy, which appeared in Eastern Europe among the population exposed to Ochratoxin-A through contaminated food. According to studies, high level of incidences of kidney and the urinary tract cancers have occurred in people afflicted with this disease, thereby proving that Ochratoxin-A can cause kidney cancer in humans. There is evidence that Ochratoxin-A is genotoxic and may cause damage to DNA, which can increase the risk of cancer, although how this occurs is unclear.

Cornell University's study found a possible connection between testicular cancer and consumption of food products contaminated by Ochratoxin-A, although no conclusions can be drawn based on this study.

Currently, there is a growing concern regarding Ochratoxin-A contamination in foods and beverages; however, not all countries test coffee. There are reported cases of highly contaminated coffee beans in amounts of 360 micrograms per kilogram (one kilogram is equal to 2.2 pounds; one pound is equal to 453, 6 grams) in the U.S.

Since 2005, Ochratoxin-A has been strictly regulated in the European Union, whereas no standards have been developed in the U.S. There are laboratories in the U.S. that can test coffee beans, but the FDA has not yet determined suggested limits regarding Ochratoxin-A contamination.

Acrylamide Is in Your Cup

Acrylamide is a toxic chemical that is found in coffee, but it is not a natural compound of the bean. Acrylamide is formed during the roasting process. It is also found, and in large amounts, in fried and baked carbohydrates such as potatoes, breads, pastries, some cereals, and grain-based coffee substitutes.

Although brewed coffee contains significantly less acrylamide than roasted whole beans or ground, it is important to change the diet because acrylamide is a carcinogen.[33] Considering that acrylamide can be consumed from other food sources too, its accumulation in the body and detrimental effects can be significant.

According to a Dutch study, after 11 years of follow-up research, the researchers discovered 327 cases of endometrial cancer, 300 cases of ovarian cancer, and 1,835 cases of breast cancer in women who consumed foods high in acrylamide.[34]

The Food and Drug Administration conducted a survey to determine acrylamide levels in some popular food products. The following FDA's chart displays some samples of the acrylamide content in roasted beans and brewed coffees. For more information on other food products containing acrylamide visit the FDA's website.

Acrylamide Values in Food Product Samples

(the data was collected between November 15, 2002 and October 1, 2004)

Acrylamide (ppb)
Maxwell House Slow Roast (ground, not brewed) 209
Starbucks Coffee Columbia Ground (ground, not brewed) 175
Folgers Classic Decaf Coffee Crystals (crystals, not brewed) 351
Maxwell House Instant Coffee (powder, not brewed) 263
Chock full o' Nuts All-Method Grind, Lot 1 (ground, not brewed) 205
Chock full o' Nuts All-Method Grind, Lot 2 (ground, not brewed) 186
Chock Ml o' Nuts 100% Colombian Coffee (ground, not brewed) 245
Folgers Classic Roast (medium roast), Lot 1 (ground, not brewed) 374
Folgers Classic Roast (medium roast), Lot 2 (ground, not brewed) 353
Folgers Classic Roast (medium roast), Lot 3 (ground, not brewed) 350
Folgers Classic Decaf (medium roast), Lot 1 (ground, not brewed) 312

Folgers Classic Decaf (medium roast), Lot 2 (ground, not brewed) 361
Folgers Classic Decaf (medium roast), Lot 3 (ground, not brewed) 326
Hills Bros Coffee, Lot 1 (ground, not brewed) 191 Hills Bros Coffee, Lot 2 (ground, not brewed) 149
Hills Bros 100% Colombian Coffee (ground, not brewed) 64
Maxwell House Master Blend (ground, not brewed) 215
Maxwell House Original Signature Blend, Lot 1 (ground, not brewed) 250
Maxwell House Original Signature Blend, Lot 2 (ground, not brewed) 170
Maxwell House Original Signature Blend Decaf Lot 1 (ground, not brewed) 222
Maxwell House Original Signature Blend Decaf, Lot 2 (ground, not brewed) 258
Melitta Traditional Premium Roast coffee (ground, not brewed) 332
Sanka Decaffeinated Coffee, Lot 1 (ground, not brewed) 351
Sanka Decaffeinated Coffee, Lot 2 (ground, not brewed) 244
Starbucks Coffee Breakfast Blend (ground, not brewed) 161
Starbucks Coffee House Blend (ground, not brewed) 151
French Market Restaurant Blend Coffee and Chicory (ground, not brewed) 609
Community Coffee & Chicory New Orleans Blend (ground, not brewed) 459
Luzianne Coffee & Chicory (ground, not brewed) 380
Cafe Regil Rige Y Regira 100% Coffee (ground, not brewed) 203
7-Eleven Regular Coffee (brewed) 5
Eleven French Roast Coffee (brewed) 6
Dunkin' Donuts Coffee Regular (brewed) 10
McDonald's Regular Coffee (brewed) 8
Starbucks Coffee Colombia (brewed) 7

The important point to remember right now is that coffee contains carcinogens and drinking coffee has been linked in various studies to increased risks for developing breast, pancreatic, bladder, lungs, and liver cancers, although the evidence that coffee causes any of these diseases is, at best, tenuous. More research needs to be performed. However, for the health conscious public, it is already perfectly clear that the link between excessive coffee consumption and diseases does exist and will become more recognized when additional research is completed.

Chapter Ten

Are You Hooked on Coffee?

Sometimes in life, the most obvious conclusions are the most difficult to accept. This seems to be particularly true with respect to our judgments concerning addictions to drugs that are, after all, legal.

For years, nicotine dependence was regarded as simply a bad smoking habit. And our viewpoints were bolstered by that infamous group of tobacco executives who told the congressional committee that "cigarette smoking is not addictive." Alcoholism was excused as a drinking problem, and it was seldom described as what it truly is: an acute chronic disease that kills many of its victims.

Likewise, caffeine addiction was formerly met with relentless denial, and insouciance by the media, even though millions of its consumers were – and still are – addicted to this stimulant. Most addicts do not realize that their "love for coffee" has deeper roots than just an innocent dietary preference.

Your Greatest Concern

The first question that comes to mind to everyone who reads this book is likely to be and, indeed, ought to be, "Am I hooked?" The answer to this question is simple: only you can tell. However, even more importantly in this age of nutritional enlightenment is whether you can quit this devil's brew.

Being hooked on coffee is not necessarily a simple numbers game. Drinking four to six cups of coffee a day, or even eight cups a day, does not automatically mean you are an addict. Nor are you automatically exonerated if you drink only a cup or two of coffee per day. The defining question to ask yourself is whether coffee has become a harmful dependence for you, regardless of the amount you drink. Is coffee causing physical or psychological disturbances to your health? Do you depend on coffee daily in order to gain some sense of physical well-being?

If your answer to these questions is no, chances are that coffee is not ensnaring you in the addictive process yet. You can probably take it or leave it as you like. If your answer to these questions is yes, you are definitely addicted to coffee. To help you decide for sure, let us first talk about your coffee habit: your consumption, your coffee-related health problems, and your dependence.

Are You Dependent on Coffee?

The first step to help you decide whether you are chemically dependent on caffeine is to measure your coffee intake. How much coffee do you drink each day? Higher levels suggest coffee dependence. However, the effect of caffeine depends not only on dosage but also on body weight, and therefore, the same amount of coffee may affect people differently. But regardless of your daily consumption, if you experience cravings for coffee, you are definitely dependent on this stimulant.

Two cups of coffee per day is what most people can safely tolerate. A study, conducted by Drs. Avram Goldstein and Sophia Kaiser at the Stanford University School of Medicine, found that it takes five or more cups of coffee per day to create a physical dependence in most people. This means that millions of people are addicted to coffee. Millions who drink five or more cups of coffee per day double the medically accepted guidelines. Our society is on a drug binge of truly epidemic proportions, and most of the victims do not even know it.

How Much Caffeine Do You Consume?

Most research suggests that people tend to minimize their actual caffeine consumption. Perhaps many coffee drinkers are vaguely aware that their beverage of choice is hazardous if it is consumed in excess, and therefore, they tend to underestimate their consumption in an effort to rationalize the shabby treatment of their bodies. However, even if they honestly tried to determine how much caffeine they consume, it would be difficult without guidelines.

Good to the Last

Consider for a moment the imprecise measurement called the cup. There is an exceedingly wide variety of coffee cups and mugs on the commercial and institutional markets these days, varying considerably in their capacities.

A dainty demitasse served at formal dinner tables is likely to contain about five ounces of coffee, maybe less. Heavy coffee drinkers, when left to their own less formal devices, usually opt for a somewhat larger cup, perhaps because it helps to eliminate trips to the coffeepot. The common household mug holds about eight ounces. But there are many super mugs on the market: as much for novelty as for coffee freaks. These mugs hold anywhere from ten to twenty ounces of coffee.

Which one do you use? Chances are that you use several different sizes. You may start the day with your favorite coffee mug at home, probably an eight-ounce cup, containing between six or seven ounces of coffee if you do not fill it to the brim. You may switch to a larger or smaller cup at work, at a restaurant, at a friend's house, or at some place else.

The only way to determine your caffeine intake is to gain a better understanding of not how many cups or ounces of coffee you drink, but how many milligrams of caffeine you consume. If you are like most coffee drinkers, you will find that you are drinking a good deal more coffee than you might have believed, posing a great risk to your well-being.

Brewing Methods Are Important

There are two more variables that complicate the issue. One is the method you choose to prepare your coffee, and the second is the length of time you allow the coffee to brew. Research has revealed that brewing preferences affect the amount of caffeine in the coffee you drink. In one study, coffee prepared by the drip-brew method contained twice as much caffeine as instant coffee.

Research suggests that the longer the brewing process, the more caffeine is extracted from coffee. The results show that just five extra minutes of brewing time can increase the caffeine in your cup from three to fourteen percent.

Coffee prepared by the drip-brew method contains approximately 128 percent more caffeine than the instant-freeze-dried coffee brands. However, coffee prepared in a percolator contains much more caffeine than coffee prepared by the drip-brew method. It makes a great deal of difference, then, what kind of coffee you are pouring into your system.

In a study, conducted at the University of Florida's College of Medicine, researchers analyzed 16-ounce servings of coffee from specialty shops and found almost twice as much caffeine, 259 milligrams, in the strongest Starbucks regular brew when compared to the weakest Dunkin Donuts® regular, containing only 143 milligrams. The decaffeinated coffees all contained less than 18 milligrams of caffeine per 16-ounce serving. The U.S. Food and Drug Administration currently does not require decaffeinated coffee to be absolutely caffeine-free.

Why Is Coffee Dangerous?

Millions of people are past the danger point and are, as the numbers show, addicted to coffee. The addiction inferred from excessive consumption and therefore excessive tolerance.

Tolerance, as indicated earlier, is one of the variables that is used to determine coffee addiction. For millions of coffee drinkers, one or two cups are simply not enough. They have to consume increasingly large amounts of coffee to obtain the feeling of well-being that they seek. Their bodies become more tolerant to higher levels of caffeine. A growing tolerance to caffeine is the same problem of tolerance that causes thousand-dollar-a-week drug addictions and pack-and-a-half-a-day cigarette habits. Without these higher levels of drug intake, the addict begins to suffer from painful and discomforting withdrawal symptoms. This discomfort, in turn, helps to perpetuate the habit because the addict seeks relief from distress by taking more of his drug of choice. For coffee addicts, daily doses exceeding nine cups seem routine. Such tolerance and habituation develop when the substance is chronically abused.

Thus, it is easy to dismiss the arguments of those who claim that if you drink 15 to 20 cups of anything, you may well suffer adverse effects. This proposition is patently untrue and also academic. What is more relevant to this hypothesis is the rarity that anyone will drink 20 cups of hot chocolate, milk, orange juice, or apple cider on a daily basis. But millions of people drink coffee at these unhealthy amounts because of its addictive qualities, and not because of any intrinsic physiological or nutritional value. They are hooked on coffee in a way that only occurs with addictive drugs.

Where Is the Real Danger Point?

Many of our personal experiences teach us about the harmful effects of coffee. Professional literature on the subject is also replete with studies that show detrimental effects of coffee on our minds and bodies.

Research has uncovered hundreds of coffee drinkers who through their own experimentation became aware that coffee was ruining their lives and decided to quit. Thousands of us are making this discovery each day. However, millions more are not sure. The bitter prognoses do not convince them, and it is understandable. People have a tendency to think that nothing will happen to them; it is always with somebody else. Their own bodies are not crying out with ailments seeking immediate relief, and research is also not clear on the exact role that coffee plays in the pathologies.

Addicts have a wide range of tolerance for coffee. Many of them can drink ten or twenty cups of coffee per day without overt complaint. However, some coffee drinkers experience throbbing headaches, palpitations, and tremulousness only after a cup or two per day. So where is the real danger point? It is at whatever a point coffee begins to adversely affect your mind or your body – regardless of whether you are aware of it.

Many of the medical risks of caffeine addiction may manifest themselves later in life while others can be seen crystal clear right away simply by quitting. Forget the rationalizations, the excuses, and quit. On Monday, right? Well, maybe you should stop delaying. You know it does not work. When Monday comes, you postpone it to the next week, then the next, and the next. Don't procrastinate it, just do it. If you are unsure about whether you are hooked, you will find out shortly after you quit. You will discover the final truth about what this drug has been doing to you all these years.

If you can quit without experiencing withdrawal symptoms, you are probably not addicted to caffeine. Many men and women who quit drinking coffee after a steady habit of anywhere from one to two cups per day do not experience withdrawal. However those who consume too much coffee usually do go through painful withdrawal symptoms after they quit.

If after going without coffee for two or three weeks you can honestly say you do not feel any better, possibly, it was not significantly affecting your mind and body. Is it possible? Most likely not. Whether you are addicted to caffeine or not, coffee is still a toxic beverage that is gradually damaging your health.

Chapter Eleven

Breaking Free From Coffee

The overwhelming preponderance of evidence, both historical and contemporary, suggests in no uncertain terms that coffee drinking is dangerous to one's health – particularly in amounts of three or more cups per day. If you are drinking more, you are damaging your health. But coffee can be injurious to health even if it is consumed in small amounts.

One day, every coffee drinker will wake up and realize the great medical dangers caused by coffee addiction and decide to quit. Coffee addicts have seen first-hand how their habit damages their minds and bodies and how this drug causes considerable pain and suffering.

Those who decided to quit obviously came to this conclusion through the pain and suffering due to their caffeine addiction. They made up their minds and no longer want this liquid devoid of nutrition and fraught with danger. While medical, clinical, and governmental institutions drag their collective feet on indicting the drug, those who decided to quit are doing it largely on their own initiative, and more power to them. No doctor, no report, no study could convince them more that coffee might have something to do with their multitudinous complaints. And most likely they would never conceive a possibility of returning to the drug, regardless of how some future study might somehow partially exonerate coffee of this or that symptom Coffee victims know the truth, and their decision to quit is worth repeating.

The Reasons to Quit

According to one study, the most prevalent out of all reasons to quit is the desire to escape from the distressing disturbances of the central nervous system. Nearly four out of ten coffee drinkers quit for this reason alone. Although central nervous system disorders are the most common problems that lead many heavy coffee drinkers to decision to quit, there are many other serious reasons. Former coffee drinkers also mention the following:

- skin problems;
- wanted to improve my health;
- concerned about breast cancer;
- palpitations;
- high blood pressure;
- heart disease;
- insomnia;
- gastrointestinal problems;
- stomach ulcers;
- admitted addiction; and
- fibrocystic breast tumors.

Whatever is your reason to quit, you have to have a strong commitment to break your caffeine dependence if you are going to make the great coffee break.

Is It Difficult to Quit?

To quit drinking coffee is relatively easy, once the commitment has been made to lead a healthy life.

Without this commitment, the memory of positive emotions from drinking coffee in the past will keep you addicted to this stimulant forever.

Most sources describe coffee as mildly addictive; however, some addicts are hooked on their drug of choice so severely that it greatly interferes with their home, work, and social life. These are the same criteria to determine if a person is an alcoholic. If the drug interferes with any of these three areas, and the addict continues to take the drug, it will lead to problems.

However, many coffee drinkers quit without the sort of problems that many heavy drug users experience. In fact, some coffee addicts are pleasantly surprised that they could quit so easily, although it is not easy for everyone. The more coffee one consumes daily, the more difficult to quit.

Something About Withdrawal

Nothing is more mysterious in coffee addiction than variances in withdrawal symptoms that accompany those who want to quit. The reactions are so varied that it is difficult to forecast whether you will suffer from withdrawal. Some experience withdrawal, some do not. Some coffee drinkers experience extremely painful withdrawal; others report relatively mild symptoms. However what is mild to one is painful to another.

Unbearable Headaches

The most universal symptom of withdrawal is a headache that is especially painful and difficult to treat medically. When the late former talks show host and Jeopardy game show creator, Merv Griffin, quit coffee, he said that his headaches were so severe that he was nearly hospitalized.

Another coffee addict said, "I got headaches for four days like I thought I was going to die." A 49-year-old woman who reported drinking ten cups of coffee a day for eight years told researchers, "It felt like the top of my head was being squeezed in a vice and I was so depressed." Another woman said that she had suffered from severe headaches for two months. A 48-year-old woman who had been drinking 9 cups of coffee for 30 years said that she experienced the worst headache she ever had in her life. "I was too sick to take anything," she said, "I just crawled in bed and just about passed out."

Not only can the headaches be extremely painful, but are also practically immune to traditional therapies. Coffee, of course, can relieve headaches almost instantly, but this is hardly a solution if you want to quit.

Other Withdrawal Symptoms

In addition to headaches, there is a long list of other withdrawal symptoms that you can experience after you quit drinking coffee. Among the universally reported maladies are lethargy, lightheadedness, sleeplessness, nervousness, tremulousness, depression, severe upset stomach, excitability, dizziness, diarrhea, grouchiness, irritability, tenseness, nausea, fever, chills, and weakness. In addition, people genuinely crave coffee.

There is very little you can do about withdrawal symptoms. Most of our respondents just suffered through the pain. Some tried analgesics, which contained caffeine, and they recovered almost instantly, but at the risk of future misery.

Selecting Your "I Quit" Day

When you decide to quit drinking coffee, make it easier for yourself. Plan your quit day in advance. If you are like most coffee drinkers, you probably drink fewer cups on the weekends. So why not plan your quit day on a weekend? If you suffer from withdrawal, you will at least be in a position to ease the symptoms.

The most difficult part is always taking that first step, but everyone can do it. If you plan your quit day on a weekend, try to pick a weekend when you do not expect to be busy. Exercise can aggravate headaches or any other withdrawal symptoms you may experience, therefore avoid physical activity.

Most likely on Monday when it is time to go back to work, you will be over some of your withdrawal symptoms and more ready to handle the week without coffee. You will already know how to face the work-day mornings without your precious cup. You will already know how to handle a certain level of work without coffee breaks. You will be prepared.

Helpful Advice

There is a trick that can help to ease the transitional period. The physical act of bringing a cup of coffee to the mouth is a formed habit and, therefore, part of the addiction. If you continue this physical act, psychologically, it will be easier to quit. Try substitute coffee with another hot beverage. Drinking something else instead of coffee will help to reduce withdrawal symptoms. Coffee addicts enjoy – and are also addicted to – the sensation of hot. Any hot beverage, even hot water, will reduce cravings for coffee.

Cold Turkey or Taper off?

Whether you quit on the weekend or during the week, you may wish to consider tapering off your coffee consumption rather than undertaking the abrupt and total withdrawal of caffeine suggested by the term "cold turkey."

If you decide to taper off, consider taking your coffee half regular and half decaf. This way, you may avoid the headaches and anxiety. You will be getting less than half of your usual caffeine intake. This way you can cut back on your coffee intake and probably avoid some withdrawal symptoms.

However, there are pros and cons in both methods. If you choose to taper off, you may avoid severe withdrawal symptoms but delay or even never reach your final goal – to quit drinking coffee. The method of "cold turkey" provides the immediate result, but it may not be easy; you may experience severe withdrawal symptoms.

Use Your Mental Power

Your mind does not know the difference between an event that happened in reality and the one that you imagined. You can imagine something and believe that it happened in reality. When you desperately want a cup of coffee, imagine that you just now finished drinking a large cup. Convince yourself that you drink too much coffee and want to reduce your consumption, but do not allow your mind to dwell upon the thought of quitting drinking coffee completely.

Psychologically, it is easier and less painful to convince yourself that you want to reduce your coffee intake and do not intend to quit drinking coffee completely. Despite the cravings, convince yourself that you just finished drinking a cup of coffee. You drink too much coffee, and it is never enough. You cannot drink cup after cup.

Your mind can hold only one thought at a time. When you think of how badly you want coffee, immediately switch your mind to the thought that you just now, at this moment, finished drinking a cup. You cannot drink another one right now because you want to reduce your coffee intake. To increase your power of resistance, think of side effects: excessive coffee consumption is harmful for your health.

Your cravings for coffee will gradually reduce and then completely disappear. In approximately two or three weeks you will have no desire to drink coffee, but it may be difficult in the beginning, especially in social situations. You may not find support and relapse; therefore, do not tell anyone that you are trying to quit. To withstand temptation, use your mental power. The right thoughts will support you. If someone will offer you a cup of coffee, you know what to say: I just had one.

This method is very effective and can help to quit not only drinking coffee but also smoking and other addictions. It can also be used for controlling appetite.

Coffee: Will You Miss It?

In various surveys, most former coffee drinkers reported that they did not miss coffee after they had endured withdrawal symptoms that accompanied their cessation. In one survey, about 90 percent of former coffee drinkers said that they did not miss it. Only those who were seriously addicted to it craved a cup of hot coffee.

How You Are Going to Feel

The most exciting discovery you are likely to make after you quit drinking coffee is how great it feels to live without it. Whether you are aware or not, coffee does affect your health and social well-being, and once your natural self has been reborn, it is easy to see what you have been missing.

Many former coffee addicts reported that once they quit drinking coffee, they were blessed with the most refreshing, deep sleep they ever experienced. These reports were received from former coffee drinkers who previously had no complaints whatsoever about their sleep. In other words, they had never really known what a good night's rest was until they quit drinking coffee.

The same is true for your general well-being. Coffee consumers often perceive themselves as calm, rational, easygoing types, until they quit drinking coffee. Then they realize that their mood swings, irritability, and jumpiness were caused by their addiction to coffee. They became aware of their problem behaviors only after they quit drinking coffee. This is one of the reasons why coffee is such an insidious drug. It places a tremendously unhealthy burden on millions of its users, and the victims often do not even know it.

Doctors also seldom question their patients about their coffee consumption And patients often withhold this information from their doctors. Thus, millions of patients endure pain and suffering, and neither doctors nor patients know that coffee is the cause of their complaints.

Healthy Alternatives to Coffee

Even before you quit drinking coffee, you are likely to worry about what you are going to drink to fill that void. This void is scary. It feels like you are losing your best friend. But in reality, life without coffee is not as terrible as you might think. Millions of former coffee drinkers indulge in other beverages after they quit their elixir. You may be astonished to learn that when most coffee drinkers quit their habit, they do not even switch to decaf. They switch to

Juice	27%
Coffee Substitutes	24%
Soft Drinks	23%
Herbal Teas	9%
Tea (Caffeinated)	5.5%
Water	4.5%
Milk/Soy/Goat	4%
Nothing	3%

(Source: Caffeine Awareness Association 2013)

A Parting Thought

Good health is one of the main components without which you will be unable to reach your life's full potential. You do not think about this when you are healthy, but you constantly dwell upon it when you are not.

You have gained a sufficient insight into the dangers of coffee and can change your life. Your decision will have significant consequences for your present and future health. Why not quit drinking coffee today? Good luck and long life.

Endnotes

Chapter One
1. Ullius K., M.D., Ptacek, G. *Age Right,* Simon & Schuster, 1999.
2. D. C. Mackay and J.W Rollins, "Caffeine and caffeinism," Journal of the Royal Naval Medical Service, 1989; 75(2):65-7
3. Girl overdoses on espresso coffee http://newsvote.bbc.co.uk
4. James Parker, The Influence of Caffeine on Kidney Stones; 1888articles; http://www.1888articles.com/the-influence-of-caffeine-on-kidney-stones-Om36sg5z39.html
5. Ajavi, O.B., Ukwade, M.T., "Caffeine and intraocular pressure in a Nigerian population," J. Glaucoma, Feb., 2002; 11(1):76
6. Monique H.M. Vlak, M.D., Gabriel J.E. Rinkel, M.D., PhD, Paut Greebe, RN, PhD, Johanna G. van der Born, M.D., PhD, Ale Algra, M.D., PhD "Trigger Factors and Their Attributable Risk for Rupture of Intracranial Aneurysm" Utrecht Stroke Center, Department of Neurology, University Medical Center, Utrecht, Netherlands, 2011

Chapter Four

7. Houessou et al., Effect of roasting conditions on the polycyclic aromatic hydrocarbon content in ground Arabica coffee and coffee brew. J.Agric.Food Chem. http://www.coffee-tea.co.uk/roasting-aromatic-compounds.php
8. Ingram Cass M.D. *Natural Cures for Killer Germs,* Knowledge House, 2004; pp. 295-296.

Chapter Five

9. Dlugosz, L. et al. Caffeine intake and spontaneous abortion, Epidemiology, May 1996; 7 (3):250-255.
10. Caffeine intake and spontaneous abortion, Journal of the American Medical Association, Feb.14, 2001; v285 i6 p713.
11. Wisborg, K., Kesmodel, U., Bech, B. H., Hedegaard, M., Henriksen, T. B. "Maternal consumption of coffee during pregnancy and still-birth and infant death in first year of life: prospective study," B.M.J., 2003; 326:420.
12. Caffeine consumption and the risk of fetal death, American Journal of Epidemiology, November 15, 2005; 162(10):983-990
13. Review: Caffeine and Birth Defects; Nutrition Research Newsletter, 1995
14. Holroyd-Leduc, J.M., Straus, S.E. "Management of urinary incontinence in women," Journal of the American Medical Association, 2004; 291:986-995.

Chapter Six

15. Biaggioni, I., Paul, S., Puckett, A., Arzubiaga, C. "Caffeine and theophylline as adenosine receptor antagonists in humans" J. Pharmacol. Exp. Thera., 1991; 258:588-593
16. Caffeine exacerbates sleep problems, Journal of the American Geriatrics Society, 1995; 43: 860-864

17. Drake, C., Jefferson, C., Roehrs, T., Roth, T. "Dose-related sleep disturbances induced by coffee and caffeine" Clin Pharmacol Tuer. 1977 Feb; 21(2):244
18. Shilo, L., Sabbah, H., Hadari, R., Kovatz, S., Weinberg, U., Dolev, S., Dagan, Y., Shenkman, L. "The effects of coffee consumption on sleep and melatonin secretion," Department of Medicine C, Meir Hospital, Sapir Medical Center, and the Sackler School of Medicine, Tel-Aviv University, 2002
19. Omvik, S. et al. "Nighttime thoughts in high and low worriers: reaction to caffeine induced sleeplessness," Behavior Respiratory Therapy, April, 2007; 45(4):715-27
20. Caffeine withdrawal symptoms attack patients after surgeries, Tufts University Diet & Nutrition Letter, Jan.,1997, v14nl1 p7 [2]

Chapter Seven

21. Weinmann, S., Siscovick, D.S., Raghunathan, T.E. et al. "Caffeine Intake in Relation to the Risk of Primary Cardiac Arrest" Epidemiology, September, 1997; 8(5):505-508.
22. Baylin, A. "Transient exposure to coffee as a trigger of a first non-fatal myocardial infarction," Department of Community Health, Brown University, Providence, Epidemiology, 2006, September; 17(5):506-11.
23. Stensvold, N., Tverdal, A., Jacobsen, B. K. "Cohort Study of Caffeine Intake and Death from Coronary Heart Disease over 12 Years," B.M.J., Mar. 2, 1996; 312 (7030): 544: 545
24. American Heart Association's Scientific Sessions 2005; www.Americanheart.org

Chapter Nine

25. "Associations between black tea and coffee consumption and risk of lung cancer among current and former smokers," Nutrition and Cancer, 2005; 52(1):15-21.

26. Warshawsky, D. Polycyclic Aromatic Hydrocarbons in Carcinogenesis, Environmental Health Perspectives, Volume 107, Number 4, April 1999
27. "Coffee habit in men linked to bladder cancer," Food Navigator, Science and Nutrition, 2004; http://www.foodnavigator.com/Science/Coffee-habit-in-men-linked-to-bladder-cancer
28. "Are coffee, tea, and total fluid consumption associated with bladder cancer risk? Results from the Netherlands Cohort Study," Cancer Causes Control. 2001 Apr;12(3):231-8.
29. "Coffee and tea consumption and cancers of the bladder, colon, and rectum," Eur. J. Cancer Prev. 2002Apr;11(2):137-45.
30. Warshawsky, D. Polycyclic Aromatic Hydrocarbons in Carcinogenesis, Environmental Health Perspectives, Volume 107, Number 4, April 1999, http://www.ehponline.org/docs/1999I107-4/ warshawsky-full.html
31. Ishitani, K. M.D.,Ph.D.,Lin, J.,Ph.D., Manson, J.E.,M.D. Ph.D., Buring, J.E., ScD, Zhang, S.M., M.D., ScD, "Caffeine consumption and the risk of breast cancer in large prospective cohort of women," Archive of Internal Medicine, October 2008;168(18):2022-2031.
32. "Ochratoxin-A: Its Cancer Risk and Potential for Exposure," Heather Clark, Ph.D., and Suzanne Snedeker, Ph.D., Cornell Program on Breast Cancer and Environmental Risk Factors, Cornell University, 2005.
33. Rice, J.M. "The carcinogenicity of acrylamide," Mutation Research/Genetic Toxicology and Environmental Mutagenesis 580 (1-2): 3-20 (2005)
34. Hogervorst, J.D., Schouten, L.J. et al. "A prospective study of dietary acrylamide intake and the risk of endometrial,ovarian, and breast cancer," Cancer. Epidem Biomarkers.Prev. 16 (11): 2304 2313. Doi:l0.1158/1055-9965

BIBLIOGRAPHY

"Anxiety and panic: Gaining control over how you're feeling," Retrieved April 4, 2005, from http://familydoctor.org/013.xml

Anxiety treatment. Retrieved April 4, 2005, from http://www.anxietyaustralia.com.au/treatment/nutrition.shtml

Biggest aggravators of the anxiety condition. Retrieved April 2, 2005, from http://www.anxietybusters.com/

Birth defects and miscarriages. Retrieved April 4, 2005, from http://www.cspinet.org/

Botella, P. and A. Parra. "Coffee increases state anxiety in males but not in females," Hum. Psychopharmacol., 2003, Mar.,18; (2):141-3.

Break free from coffee. Retrieved April 1, 2005, from http://www.twilightbridge.com/deaddictions/coffee.htm

Brown, S.E.,Triveri,L.,Jr. "The Acid Alkaline Food Guide," 2006

Cigarette together with a coffee super bad for your heart. Retrieved April 1, 2005, from http://www.medicalnewstoday.com/medicalnews.php?newsid=16343

Cigarettes and coffee may not be the perfect blend. Retrieved April 1, 2005, from http://www.bupa.co.uk/healthinformation/html/health/news/121104coffeecigarettesheart.html

Clay, R. "Coffee brews trouble for the naturally nervous," Retrieved Caffeine Bibliography April 4, 2005, from http://archives.cnn.com/2000/HEALTH/diet.fitness/07/07/java.iive.wmd/index.html

Coffee can damage teeth. Retrieved April 1, 2005, from http://www.menshealth.co.uk/

Coffee can raise cholesterol, American Journal of Epidemiology, February 15, 2001; 153: 353362.

Coffee, high blood pressure linked to stroke, Journal of Clinical Epidemiology, 1998; 51:487-494.

Coffee in strokes danger. Retrieved April 1, 2005, from http://www.dailyrecord.co.uk/

Coffee in the morning, stress later on. Retrieved April 1, 2005, from http://www.accaglobal.com/

Coffee may damage blood vessels, 22nd Congress of the European Society of Cardiology, August, 2000

Coffee may pump up work stress. Retrieved April 4, 2005, from http://www.healthday.com/

Coffee pregnancy warning. Retrieved April 2, 2005, from http://news.bbc.co.uk/2/hi/health/2780695.stm

Cure for Caffeine Allergy; Home Remedies; Health & Nutrition, 2010 http://www.herbal-home-remedies.com/blog/420/cure-for-caffeine-allergy/

Davis, J. "Coffee break can break your diet," Retrieved April 4, 2005, from http://my.webmd.com/content/article/61/67392.htm

Eaton, WW, McLeod, J. "Consumption of coffee or tea and symptoms of anxiety," Am. J. Public. Health 1984;74:66-68

Fife, B., Doctor of Naturopathic Medicine: Are you eating rancid oils

Freestone, S., Ramsay, L.E. "Effect of coffee and cigarette smoking on the blood pressure of untreated and diuretic-treated hypertensive patients," Am. J. Med., 1982; 73:348-353.

Gregory, S.J. "A Holistic Protocol for the Immune System: HIV IARC/ AIDS/Candidiasis/EpsteinBarr/Herpes and other opportunistic infections,"1995.

Griffiths, R.R., Ph.D., The Johns Hopkins University School of Medicine, Professor of Behavioral Biology, Department of Psychiatry & Behavioral Sciences, Professor of Neuroscience, Department of Neuroscience, Third Edition (pp. 193-224)

Grubben, M.J., Boers, G.H., Blom, H.J., Broekhuizen, R., de Jong, R., van Rijt, L., de Ruijter, E., Swinkels, D.W, Nagengast, F.M., and Katan, M.B. "Unfiltered coffee increases plasma homocysteine concentrations in healthy volunteers: a randomized trial," American Journal of Clinical Nutrition, 2000, 71(2):480-4.

Hiatt R.A., Klatsky, A.L., Armstrong, M.A., Pancreatic cancer, blood glucose and beverage consumption; International Journal of Cancer, 2006 http://onlinelibrary.wiley.com/doi/10.1002/ijc.2910410603/abstract

Hitti, M. "Coffee may raise heart disease risk," Retrieved April 4, 2005, from http://my.webmd.com/content/article/95/103424.htm

Ingri Harkins, Coffee: pure poison to our digestive tract; Idaho Observer, 2006 http://proliberty.com/observer/20001011.htm

Kalmus, S., Effects of Eating Rancid Oil; http://www.livestrong.com/article/445254-effects-of-eating-rancid-oil/

Jee, S.H., He, J., Whelton, P.K., Suh, I., Klag, M.J. "The effect of chronic coffee drinking on blood pressure: a meta-analysis of controlled clinical trials," Hypertension, 1999; 33:647-652.

Kidney stones a new risk for coffee drinkers. Retrieved April 2, 2005, from http://www.mercola.com/2004/sep/22/kidneystonescoffee.htm

Lader, M., Bruce, M. "States of anxiety and their induction by drugs," Br. J. Clin. Pharmacol., 1986, Sep.;22(3):251-61

Lorenzo, N.Y. M.D., et al. Brain Aneurysm; E-Medicine Health; http://www.emedicinehealth.com/

Lynch, A., Does coffee have any effect on bladder cancer? 2011; http://www.livestrong.com/article/443959-does-coffee-have-any-effect-on-bladder-cancer

Macready, N. "No bones about it: drinking coffee may increase arthritis risk," Retrieved April 4, 2005, from http://my.webmd.com/ content/article/26/1728_59767

The medical effects of coffee, Medical World News, January 26, 1976, page 63-73.

Mercola, J. "Just one cup of coffee a day creates an addiction," Retrieved April 2, 2005, from http://www.mercola.com/2004/oct/13/coffeeaddiction.htm

Mercola, J. and Doege, R. "Coffee: How bad is it really?" Retrieved April 2, 2005, from http://www.mercola.com/2003/dee/10/coffee.htm

Miscarriage and the coffee connection, Science News, October 25, 1975; page 267.

Morning coffee boosts blood pressure, stress hormones throughout the day. Retrieved April 4, 2005, from http://www.pslgroup.com/

Pancreatic Cancer; A service of the U.S. National Library of Medicine; National Institutes of Health; http://www.nlm.nih.gov/medlineplus/pancreaticcancer.html

Panagiotakos, D.B., Pitsavos, C., Chrysohoou, C., Kokkinos, P., Toutouzas, P., and Stefanadis, C. "The J-shaped effect of coffee consumption on the risk of developing acute coronary syndromes: the CARDIO2000 case-control study," Journal of Nutrition, 2003; 133(10):3228-32.

Papamichael, C., Aznaouridis, K. et al. "Coffee exerts an acute unfavorable effect on endothelial function of healthy subjects," American Society of Hypertension annual meeting, May 18-22, 2004, New York.

Patenaude, F. "Coffee: The great energy sapper," Retrieved April 1, 2005, from http://www.fredericpatenaude.com/

Pregnancy precautions. Retrieved April 1, 2005, from http://topicsaz.parenthood.com/articles.html?article_id=3126

Raloff, J. "Cardiovascular showdown -chocolate versus coffee," Science News Online, May 29, 2004; Vol. 165, No. 22.

Reuters Health. "Coffee, cigarette combo is extra hard on arteries," Retrieved April 3, 2005, from http://www.heartcenteronline.com/myheartdr/home/research-detail.cfm?reutersid=4825

Salazar-Martinez, E., Willett, WC., Ascherio, A., Manson, J.E., Leitzmann, M.F., Stampfer, M.J., and Hu, F.B. "Coffee consumption and the risk for type 2 diabetes mellitus," Annals of Internal Medicine, 2004; 140(1):1-8.

Salvador, H.S., Koos, B.J. "Effects of regular and decaffeinated coffee on fetal breathing and heart rate," J. Obstet. Gynecol., 1989; 161:669.

Sant, G.R. "Interstitial cystitis – a urogynecologic perspective" Contemporary Obstetrics and Gynecology, 1998; 43.6:119-130

Silberstein, J.L. and J. Kellogg Parsons, Evidence-based principles of bladder cancer an diet; Urology 75:340-346, 2010

Starbucks coffee company fact sheet, February 2007. http://www.starbucks.com

Stoppler, M. "Morning coffee can stress you all day," Retrieved April 3, 2005, from http://stress.about.com/

Sun Network. (2004). "Coffee impairs short-term memory," Retrieved April 2, 2005, from http://www.mercola.com/

The effects of caffeine on the skin; http://www.skin-care-tips-online.com/

Tonda, L., Rudas, N., "The course of a seasonal bipolar disorder influenced by caffeine," Journal of Affective Disorders, 1991; 22 (4):249-251

Toxic elements of coffee roasting; http://www.coffee-tea.co.uk/Roasting.php

Tracey, E. That morning cup may help you sense fall in blood sugar. Retrieved April 4, 2005, from http://my.webmd.com/content/article/23/1728_56543

Tuomilehto, J., Hu, G., Bidel, S., Lindstrom, J., and Jousilahti, P. "Coffee consumption and the risk of type 2 diabetes mellitus among middle-aged Finnish men and women," JAMA, 2004; 291(10):1213-9. Tuomilehto, J., Tuomilehto-Wolf, E., Virtala, E., LaPorte, R. "Coffee consumption as trigger for insulin dependent diabetes mellitus in childhood," British Medical Journal, 1990; 300(6725): 642-3.

Vega Jose M.D., Ph.D., Brain Aneurysms – The Basics; About.com Health's Disease and Condition Content; Reviewed by the Medical Review Board, 2009 http://stroke.about.com/od/causesofstroke/a/aneurysm.htm

Wallace, S. "Java's Jolt Bad for Blood Pressure?" Retrieved April 2, 2005, from http://www.healthatoz.com/healthatoz/Atoz/de/cen/card/hyprIalert07122001.jsp

Warner, J. "Coffee packs more than a caffeine buzz" Retrieved April 4, 2005, from http://my.webmd.com/content/article/53/61360.htm

Winstead, Daniel K. M.D. "Coffee consumption among psychiatric inpatients," American Journal of Psychiatry, December, 1976; 133:12

What I need to know about Kidney Stones; National Kidney and Urologic Diseases Information Clearinghouse; NIH Publication No. 07-4154, April 2007

Resources

Caffeine Clinic
Johns Hopkins University School of Medicine

Johns Hopkins Bayview Campus Behavioral Biology Research Center
5510 Nathan Shock Dr.
Baltimore, MD 21224-6823
Tel: 410-550-2687 or 410-550-0007
Website: www.Caffeinedependence.org

The clinic is opened for an ongoing research study being conducted at Johns Hopkins to better characterize the caffeine addiction syndrome and to evaluate the effectiveness of a simple treatment program to help people cut back or eliminate caffeine use.

The free clinic is open to anyone who feels they are psychologically or physically dependent on caffeine (from coffee, tea, soda, or tablets) or who have tried unsuccessfully to quit caffeine use in the past. Participation involves a thorough assessment of caffeine use and a structured program for painlessly cutting back or eliminating caffeine use.

About The Author

Marina Kushner was born in Russia. She received her education at Moscow University, majoring in journalism, and worked for a major Russian newspaper *Izvestia*.

Working under the pressure of daily deadlines, Kushner, as her colleagues, made it through the day on a diet of cigarettes and coffee. Her soon-developed health problems as a result of her everyday excessive coffee intake motivated her to write a book about detrimental effects of coffee on the mind and body, which are often underreported.

Her book *The Truth About Coffee* provides important information to help consumers make informed decisions regarding consumption of this potentially dangerous beverage.

www.ingramcontent.com/pod-product-compliance
Lightning Source LLC
Chambersburg PA
CBHW070111080526
44586CB00013B/1259